Tab. VI.

Haus-Voegel.

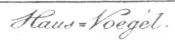

Inländische Voegel.

Ausländische Voegel.

THE ANIMAL
ILLUSTRATED
1550–1900

HARRY N. ABRAMS, INC.
PUBLISHERS, NEW YORK

THE ANIMAL ILLUSTRATED 1550–1900

∎

From the Collections of The New York Public Library

TEXT BY JOSEPH KASTNER

∎

with commentaries by Miriam T. Gross

Editor: Ruth A. Peltason
Designer: Elissa Ichiyasu

Photographs by Philip Popcock

Endpapers:
Uncolored etchings. In Naturgeschichte für Kinder . . .
by Jacob Glatz (18———).

Page 3:
Northern Birch Mouse. Etching. In Novae species quadrupedum . . .
by Peter Simon Pallas (1778–79).

Page 6:
Frontis. Hand-colored engraving. In Historia naturalis ranarum
nostratium . . . *by Augustin Roesel von Rosenhof (1758).*

Page 9:
"The Creation of Adam." In Animals in art and thought to the end
of the Middle Ages *edited by Evelyn Antal and John Harthan.*
Cambridge, Mass.: M.I.T. Press, 1971.
Illustration by Francis Donald Klingender.

Library of Congress Cataloging-in-Publication Data
Kastner, Joseph.
The animal illustrated 1550–1900
from the collections of the New York public library:
text / by Joseph Kastern;
with commentaries by Miriam T, Gross.
p.   cm.
Includes bibliographical references and index.
ISBN 0–8109–1907–9
1. Animals in art—Catalogs.
2. Illustration of books—Catalogs.
3. Books—New York (N.Y)—Catalogs.
4. New York Public Library—Catalogs.
I. Gross, Miriam T.
II. Title.
NC961.7.A54K37   1991
741.6'4'0747471—dc20   90–43754
CIP

CONTENTS

■

ADMIRANDA T
LEVIVM SPECTACVLA
RERVM

The New York Public Library is particularly pleased to share its collections for the creation of this volume, *The Animal Illustrated*, in conjunction with an exhibition mounted at the Central Research Library. The Library's collections of over 37 million catalogued items include rich holdings in illustrated plate books, tracing the development of the study of flora and fauna from all parts of the earth. While scholars have used these collections for over a century, they are among the less-known treasures of the Library's holdings. ▪ Illustrations of terrestrial, aquatic, airborne, and microscopic animals have fascinated naturalists for centuries. This volume traces the collaboration of the artist and scientist from the sixteenth through the nineteenth centuries. During this period, zoological representation attracted the attention of such renowned artists and scientists as Charles Darwin, Count Buffon, and Titian Ramsey Peale. Their art, executed in the forms of colored and uncolored woodcuts, wood engravings, metal engravings, and lithographs forged a partnership between two great disciplines, science and art. While its primary intent was to represent the animal as accurately as possible, we have come to regard many of these illustrations as works of art as well. For

▪

FOREWORD
BY
TIMOTHY S. HEALY

▪

President

The New York Public Library

The Animal Illustrated, some of the more visually striking images were chosen from the collections of the Library. ▪ The development of a book and exhibition has provided the Library an extraordinary opportunity to conserve some of the great plate books whose illustrations grace this volume. This has allowed us to preserve the record of the past for the delight and enjoyment of present and future generations. ▪ The Library would like to acknowledge the sustained and diligent efforts of Miriam Gross, a reference librarian of the Library's General Research Division, whose abiding passion for the illustrated book has led to this exhibition on the animal illustrated. ▪ The Library also wishes to recognize the support of Bulgari and the Vincent Astor Foundation in the preparation of the book and the exhibition. The generosity of the sponsors has been the sine qua non for the development of these projects. ▪ And finally, a word of thanks to Harry N. Abrams, Inc., with whom the Library has worked to produce several volumes that document the art and science of zoological and botanical illustration. Through these publications the Library is able to share collections with audiences who may not otherwise have the opportunity to discover the Library or its exhibitions.

A PEACEABLE KINGDOM OF BOOKS AND ART

Around the year 1100, the monks at the monastery of Eynsham in England set themselves to the task of illustrating the Creation as recorded in Genesis. When they came to reenact the sixth day, the monks depicted the animals in the peaceable kingdom of Eden, looking on in wonder as the Lord held the body of Adam, newly shaped from the dust of paradise, at the moment when He is about to breathe life into man. In the next scene, the Creation is completed when the animals go up one by one to be given their names by Adam. ▪ In that first age of innocence, according to the preachers, man knew the animals as the Lord intended him to. But this ended with the Fall. "Since Adam went out of Paradise," wrote Edward Topsell in 1607, "there was never any that was able perfectly to describe the universal condition of all sort of beasts. Therefore," said Topsell introducing his *History of the Four-footed Beasts*, "hearken to that which I have observed." ▪ Topsell, who was both a naturalist and a minister in the Church of England, gave a pious reason for his book. But his real reason was the one which impelled all the Renaissance: to seek and spread knowledge. He was writing at the time when natural history, like so many branches of learning, was making its epic transformation from a form of accepted information and misinformation into a questioning science. A few decades before Topsell began his

History, Conrad Gesner, a physician and naturalist of Zurich, had described the universal condition of beasts with his pioneering *Historiae animalium*. A three-volume work, it was filled with illustration, as was Topsell's *History*, which borrowed freely from Gesner. ▪ More than any other branch of science, natural history has leaned on artists to explain and illuminate its findings—and, just as important, to attract readers. The early printers understood this very well—the popularity of their books was immensely increased by illustrations. The pleasure of the readers in looking at them was matched by the delight of the artists in making them and this is happily evident in the pages of *The Animal Illustrated*. ▪ The illustrations have all come from books in the collections of The New York Public Library which, in itself, is a kind of peaceable kingdom inhabited by creatures that artists have seen, or read about, or heard about, or simply imagined. The books were published between the start of the sixteenth century and the end of the nineteenth and there are familiar names among them: John Gould, the encyclopedic impresario of nature; Mark Catesby and Alexander Wilson, the early American painters of nature; Albrecht Dürer, who painted not only religious masterworks but rabbits and rhinoceri. And there are familiar names in unfamiliar roles—John James Audubon painting not birds but quadrupeds and Edward Lear portraying believable turtles instead of nonsensical storks and ravens. ▪ Western cultures and its artists did not depict animals as. gods, as other cultures did, but drew, painted, or carved them for the glory of God. They are still everywhere in the houses of Christendom. Winged lions patrol the roof of San Marco in Venice, apes peek out between the lines of medieval church manuscripts while rabbits run up the margins and doves fly into the calligraphy. Kings and saints awaited heaven in shrouds embroidered with animals—Charlemagne's adorned with elephants, St. Germain's with eagles, and St. Cuthbert's, more humbly, with ducks. ▪ The place of animals in the great scheme of things had been decreed by the Old Testament, which gave man "dominion over the fish of the sea and over the birds of the air and over everything that moves on earth." A later observer put this more

bluntly, saying that animals were "intended for the peculiar convenience of mankind." Each animal had a particular purpose. Cows and pigs were here to feed man, horses and oxen to work for him. Serpents were to remind him of his fall and there was a purpose even for lice—to make men keep themselves clean. ▪ According to the church, animals had no souls, therefore they had no rights. Since creatures without souls could not feel pain, there was no need for men to be kind to them or to be concerned, except in practical ways, for their lives. ▪ There were a few who found arrogance in these attitudes. Back in the third century, the eminent scholar Porphyry argued that man's convenience was not a reason for animal's existence. "It is as absurd," he argued, "to think that pigs were made to be eaten by man as that man was made to be eaten by crocodiles." Montaigne, the French satirist, suggested mischievously that the only thing distinguishing man "from his fellow members of the animal kingdom" was "his own vanity." ▪ It was not until the end of the eighteenth century, when the rights of man were being proclaimed, that animals were also granted some rights. The humane movement became a popular cause, enlisting everyone from politicians to poets. In Parliament, a law making cruelty to animals a crime was introduced by Lord Erskine, a former chancellor whose many pets included a goose and two leeches. And even the gentle art of fishing was attacked by Lord Byron who denounced the angler as "a cruel coxcomb" who *in his gullet/Should have a hook/And a small trout to pull it* ▪ Today, of course, the animal rights movements have turned man's thinking on animals upside down. The Bible's insistence that man has dominion over animals seems archaic. Much more suited to modern sensibility is Ecclesiastes which sees men and animals as equal. "They all have one breath," said the Preacher, "so that man has no preeminence over beast."

In somewhat the same way that people today make lists rating the greatest baseball players of all time or the best dressed women of the year, naturalists used to make up hierarchies of the earth's creatures. Having acknowledged that man was just beneath the angels, they then put the animals below him, starting with the fiercest and most powerful—the lion, the elephant, and the eagle, with the horse high up on the list because of its nobility. As the list went down, the animals generally got smaller and meeker to end with such seeming inconsequential creatures as insects and clams. ▪ Since there was a purpose for each animal, that of the fiercest beast was, as often as not, to test man's courage. Great warriors always measured themselves against the lion, the daunting king of beasts. One emperor of Assyria, Ashurbanipel, boasted that he killed a lion by splitting its head with his axe, while another emperor sought glory wholesale by killing a thousand of them. Rulers took on the lion's name as a mantle of greatness. Solomon was the "lion king," while a German prince called himself Henry the Lion and Richard I of England liked to be referred to as lion-hearted. Humbler people were more literal about being lion hearted, killing lions so they could eat the heart and thereby make themselves brave. ▪ Sometimes men flaunted their position by collecting the wildest animals. Ashurbanipel, when he wasn't axing lions, kept them in a menagerie along with tigers and camels. Frederick II, a holy Roman emperor and a renowned naturalist, traveled throughout his realms with his private zoo. His hosts, though honored to welcome their sovereign, were less pleased to have to put up his troupe of tigers and elephants. ▪ The most impressive animals were favorite subjects in the early printed books. At first, the likenesses were crude and approximate because of the limitations of the woodcut, the first method of printed reproduction. As the subtler processes of engraving and etching in metal were perfected, the art became finer and more accurate. The nineteenth century became a golden age for the art of natural history with the invention of the lithograph, a method of drawing directly on stone and transferring that image to paper. This not only gave the artist more freedom but was also a less expensive process and made possible the mass production of illustrated books. ▪ John James Audubon, who had used engravings for his *Birds of America*, switched to lithography for *The Quadrupeds of North America*. It was his last work, and included paintings by his gifted son, John Woodhouse Audubon. To gather material for *Quadrupeds*, Audubon traveled west, far up the Missouri River, where he met a stunning Indian princess named Natawista who spoke cultured French, shot wolves from her horse while riding bareback, and dove into the river to retrieve some ducks Audubon had shot. She lost some of her allure for the aging but still susceptible artist when, offering him a newly shot buffalo head as a model for a drawing, she first cracked open the skull and ate the brains raw—a particular delicacy, she explained, because they were still warm.

GREAT BEASTS OF THE WILD

1 ▪ TIGER *Panthera tigris*

"Tigris Gesneri." Woodcut. In *Opera omnia* by Ulisse Aldrovandi (1599–1668). ▪ One of the founders of modern zoology, Aldrovandi was Professor of Zoology at the University of Bologna, headed its Botanic Gardens, and established its Museum, where his papers and enormous natural history collections are still held. Only four of the fourteen volumes of his "Complete Works" were published during his lifetime; his disciples brought the work to completion. Unlike Conrad Gesner, who arranged his *Historiae animalium* alphabetically, Aldrovandi grouped his animals by type. The numerous highly attractive woodcut illustrations are integral to the text, and are usually quite accurate, although this tiger copied from Gesner is hardly more than recognizable.

THE LION TIGER CUBS,

BORN AT WINDSOR. 1824

London. Published June 1. 1830. by Moon. Boys & Graves. Printsellers to the King. 6. Pall Mall.

2 ▪ LION-TIGER HYBRID

"The Lion Tiger Cubs." Etching, by Thomas Landseer from his own drawing. In *Characteristic sketches of animals . . .* by John Henry Barrow (1832). ▪ The birth of these hybrid cubs at Windsor Park on October 17, 1824 generated great excitement for this was the first recorded observation of this phenomenon. The sire, a lion of gentle disposition bred by a Mr. Atkins, a well-known exhibitor of wild animals, acquired as companion and mate a wild-born but equally gentle tigress. The cubs are shown at three months.

THE BENGAL TIGERS.
MENAGERIE, KINGS MEWS.

3 ▪ TIGER *Panthera tigris*

"The Bengal Tigers." Etching, by Thomas Landseer from his own drawing. In *Characteristic sketches of animals . . .* by John Henry Barrow (1832). ▪ "When goaded by hunger, nothing can daunt the temerity or repress the ravages of this fierce marauder," said Barrow of the tiger, whom he also called "the scourge of an immense portion of Southern Asia." The highly dramatic text is stylistically compatible with the equally vivid depictions of London zoo inhabitants, most of whom are depicted in the wild.

4 · CHEETAH *Acinonyx jubatus*

["Felis guttata"]. Drawing with watercolor, signed "Hans, fecit." Original drawing for, or later copy of, illustration in *Die Saugethiere in Abbildungen nach der Natur . . .* by Johann Christian Daniel Schreber (1774(?)–1855(?)). ▪ Although cheetahs are the swiftest mammals—able to accelerate from 0 to 45 m.p.h. in two seconds, and clocked at over 60 m.p.h.—they tire quickly after several hundred yards. Unlike many cats, cheetahs will eat only their own kill and will abandon a carcass to other animals when their hunger is satisfied.

Katt-Lo.
(Felis cervaria) Gammal i vinterdrägt.

C.v Scheele Lithogr.   6 af nat: stl.

5 · EUROPEAN LYNX *Felis lynx*

"Katt-Lo." Hand-colored lithograph, by C. von Scheele from drawing by M. von Wright. In *Illuminerade Figurer till Skandinaviens Fauna* by Sven Nilsson (1832–40). ▪ Some two hundred illustrations by Wright and Magnus Köerner depict the animals of Scandinavia in Nilsson's great regional atlas. Here the lynx is shown in its lush winter pelage, perfectly suited to cold climates. Long legs enable it to travel quickly through snow, aided by furred foot pads which supply both traction and warmth.

LEOPARD.

ZOOLOGICAL GARDENS.

London. Published Sep.: 1, 1831, by Moon, Boys & Graves, Printsellers to the King & Pall Mall.

6 ▪ LEOPARD *Panthera pardus*

"Leopard." Etching, by Thomas Landseer from his own drawing. In *Characteristic sketches of animals . . .* by John Henry Barrow (1832). ▪ Thomas Landseer, one of the finest printmakers of his time, devoted much of his career to engraving the extremely popular animal paintings of his famous younger brother, Sir Edwin. Thomas's own skills as an animal artist were considerable and were displayed in his many illustrations for *Characteristic sketches* and other books.

FELIS LEO   *Cinquieme de la Grandeur*   LE LION.

Dedié au premier Consul   *Par le Citoyen Miger.*

7 ▪ LION *Panthera leo*

"Le Lion." Etching, by Simon Charles Miger from painting by Nicolas Maréchal. In *La Ménagerie du Muséum National d'Histoire Naturelle . . .* by Nicolas Maréchal (1801). ▪ This superb collection of animal portraits is also a revealing picture of the French political scene after the Revolution. The authors of the text, Bernard-Germain-Etienne de la ville, Le comte de Lacépède, and Baron Georges Cuvier, are cited on the title page simply as Citoyen Lacépède and Citoyen Cuvier. Many plates bear inscriptions: this etching of the so-called King of Beasts is dedicated by Citoyen Miger to the First Consul—a.k.a. Napoleon Bonaparte.

ELEPHANTUS INDICUS *Fœmina.*
L'ÉLÉPHANT DES INDES *(Femelle)*

Dixieme de la Grandeur

8 ▪ INDIAN ELEPHANT *Elephas maximas*

"L'Éléphant des Indes (Femelle)." Etching, by Simon Charles Miger from painting by Nicolas Maréchal. In *La Ménagerie du Muséum National d'Histoire Naturelle . . .* by Nicolas Maréchal (1801). ▪ Because of the Revolution, in 1793 the former Jardin du Roi and Cabinet du Roi became the plain Jardin des Plantes and Muséum National d'Histoire Naturelle. A zoological garden linked with the Muséum was also established, replacing the royal Ménagerie du Parc at Versailles. In his capacity as "Painter of the Muséum," Maréchal documented this elephant and the other animals of the new zoo in the Jardin des Plantes. His watercolor paintings on vellum became part of the enormous *collection des velins* of some 6,500 depictions of plants and animals that date back to Gaston, Duc d'Orléans in the seventeenth century.

HIPPOPOTAMUS.

9 ▪ HIPPOPOTAMUS *Hippopotamus amphibius*

"Hippopotamus." Etching, by White from drawing by Moses Griffith. In *Zoological lectures delivered at the Royal Institution . . .* by George Shaw (1809). ▪ A love of zoology prompted George Shaw to abandon the ministry. During a long and distinguished career he helped found the Linnaean Society, was associated with the British Museum's natural history section, edited the learned journal *Philosophical Transactions*, and published several finely illustrated works on natural history. The Hippopotamus in Shaw's *Lectures* has its mouth open wide, the better to show off its dangerous two-foot-long tusks, which, said Shaw, were especially prized by dentists for making false teeth. Hippo ivory, unlike that from elephants, does not discolor.

Camelopardalis Giraffa.

10 ▪ GIRAFFE *Giraffa camelopardalis*

"Camelopardalis Giraffa." Hand-colored lithograph, by J. Zeitter from drawing by Robert Hills. In *Transactions of The Zoological Society of London.* 1847–. ▪ This giraffe family depicted in the wild was actually a resident of the Zoological Society Gardens in London. The imaginary scene commemorates the first birth of a giraffe in a European menagerie. Conceived on April 1, 1838, the calf was born June 19, 1839: a gestation period of 444 days (well over fourteen months).

ZEBRA.

Designed & Engraved by W.ᵐ Daniell & Published by Mes.ʳˢ Cadell & Davies London May 1 1812.

11 · MOUNTAIN ZEBRA *Equus zebra*

"Zebra." Monochrome aquatint from his own drawing, by William Daniell. In *Interesting selections from animated nature . . .* by William Daniell (1809). ▪ Daniell evidently believed that if an animal looks like a horse it should behave like a horse, for he complained that the zebra was "vicious and indocile," attempts at taming it not yet having succeeded. Daniell tells the tale of an English dragoon who attempted to ride a zebra mare. To unseat her unwelcome burden the mare leaped from a high bank into a river. Although dislodged the dragoon still clutched the bridle and was dragged to shore, where the zebra "put her head down to his face, and completely bit off his ear."

SIMIA PETAURISTA   (Moitié de Grandeur)   LE BLANC-NEZ

12 ▪ LESSER WHITE-NOSED MONKEY *Cercopithecus petaurista*

"Le Blanc-Nez." Etching, by Simon Charles Miger from painting by Nicolas Maréchal. In *La Ménagerie du Muséum National d'Histoire Naturelle . . .* by Nicolas Maréchal (1801). ▪ These small primates belong to the group called guenons, whose genus name *Cercopithecus* is a misnomer. The Greek *pithekos* means ape, and these are monkeys. (In general, apes are tailless, while monkeys have tails.) Both monkeys and apes were favorite subjects of illustrators, who were given to emphasizing the animals' likeness to humans.

13 · GIBBON *Hylobates sp.*

Drawing with watercolor, unsigned. Original drawing for, or later copy of, illustration in *Die Saugethiere in Abbildungen nach der Natur . . .* by Johann Christian Daniel Schreber (1774(?)–1855(?)). This gibbon, an ape found in parts of Southeast Asia, appears not only in Schreber's poorly documented mammal atlas, but also in the third (1793) edition of Thomas Pennant's *History of quadrupeds.* Since over sixty artists are credited to the published engravings, it is likely that Schreber reused previously published art.

Keulemans pinx.^t

Imp Becquet fr. Paris.

Lemur catta.

14 ▪ RING-TAILED LEMUR *Lemur catta*

"Lemur catta." Chromolithograph, by Bequet from drawing by John Gerrard Keulemans. In *Histoire physique, naturelle et politique de Madagascar . . .* by Alfred Grandidier and Alphonse Milne Edwards (1875–1942). ▪ The Ring-tail is the best known of the lemurs, dog-faced prosimians found only in the forests of Madagascar. A sociable species, living in groups of five to twenty, the Ring-tails can be easily identified by their catlike ringed tails, which are held aloft as the animals move about the ground.

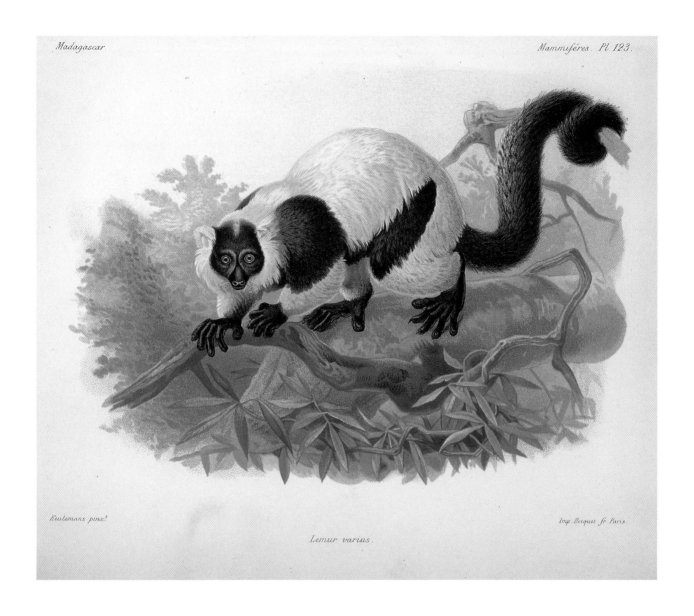

Keulemans pinx.^t   *Imp. Becquet fr. Paris.*

Lemur varius.

15 ▪ RUFFED LEMUR *Lemur variegatus*

"Lemur varius." Chromolithograph, by Bequet from drawing by John Gerrard Keulemans. In *Histoire physique, naturelle et politique de Madagascar . . .* by Alfred Grandidier and Alphonse Milne Edwards (1875–1942). ▪ Alfred Grandidier's massive study (29 volumes in 50) is based on his many years of exploration of the large island southeast of Africa, now the Malagasy Republic. While *Histoire* is certainly his greatest legacy, his name also lives on in the various Madagascar fauna and flora (including a variety of poison ivy) named for him.

Plate LVI

On Stone by Wᵐ E. Hitchcock

American Bison or Buffalo

Drawn from Nature by J.J.Audubon,F.R.S. F.L.S.

Lith. Printed & Colᵈ by J.T.Bowen, Phil.

16 • BISON *Bison bison*

"American Bison or Buffalo." Hand-colored lithograph, by William E. Hitchcock from drawing by John James Audubon. In *The quadrupeds of North America* by John James Audubon and John Bachman (1849–54). ▪ *Viviparous quadrupeds of North America*, with 150 plates, was first issued in a folio edition, 1845–48. This octavo set, with five additional illustrations, was completed and published by Audubon's family after his death in 1851. Although fully half of the illustrations for *Quadrupeds* were contributed by Audubon's son, John Woodhouse, the portraits of America's largest land mammal were by John James, who was nearly killed by one of his subjects. One Bison bull shot by Audubon and his companions turned upon his attackers, who narrowly escaped injury before the wounded animal fell.

URSUS MARITIMUS. L'OURS POLAIRE. *(sixieme de la Grandeur)*

*Dedié au Citoyen Faujas - S.^t - fond, Professeur de Géologie
au Muséum National d'histoire Naturelle, Inspecteur des Mines de France &c, par le Citoyen Miger.*

17 ▪ POLAR BEAR *Ursus maritimus*

"L'Ours Polaire." Etching, by Simon Charles Miger from painting by Nicolas Maréchal. In *La Ménagerie du Muséum National d'Histoire Naturelle . . .* by Nicolas Maréchal (1801). ▪ Polar Bears are perfectly designed for life in the Arctic, and thus would have seemed poor candidates for a life in captivity in temperate climates before zoos were able to replicate natural habitats. Yet there are reports of bears being displayed live in 1st century B.C. Egypt, and of ninth-century Vikings bringing home live specimens. In the thirteenth century a Polar Bear was brought from Greenland, via Iceland and Norway, to Palermo, Sicily, as a gift to the Holy Roman Emperor Frederick II, who had his own private zoo and was author of the classic study "The art of hunting with birds."

OSPHRANTER ANTILOPINUS; Gould.

18 ▪ ANTELOPE KANGAROO *Macropus antilopinus*

"Osphranter Antilopinus—Red Wallaroo." Hand-colored lithograph, by Henry Constantine Richter. In *A monograph of the macropodidae, or family of kangaroos* by John Gould (1841–42). ▪ *Birds of Australia* (1837–38) was John Gould's first study of the natural history of the island continent. It was illustrated from his sketches by his wife, Elizabeth, who also bore their fifth child during the sojourn down under. Elizabeth died in childbirth in 1841, and Gould acquired a new artist for his study of the kangaroos. Henry Constantine Richter worked with Gould for the next forty years and produced over 1,000 lithographed illustrations.

PETROGALE XANTHOPUS. *Gray*

19 ▪ YELLOW-FOOTED ROCK WALLABY *Petrogale xanthopus*

"Petrogale Xanthopus." Hand-colored lithograph, by John Gould and either Henry Constantine Richter or Josef Wolf. In *The mammals of Australia* by John Gould (1845–63). ▪ The second volume of Gould's three-part study of Australia's unique mammals is devoted entirely to the kangaroo family, and records species in addition to those in his earlier monograph on that subject. The scientific name of this small kangaroo derives from Greek (*petra* = rock, *xanthos* = yellow, *pous* = foot) and describes the agile wallaby exactly. Aided by rough-soled feet it can scale almost vertical cliffs on its hind legs. The model for this unsigned portrait, together with other Australian specimens, is now in the British Museum's natural history section.

Although most people do not think of themselves in that way, they are friends, neighbors, or hosts to animals classed by zoologists as domesticated and as comsensal, which means literally "sharing the table." Sometimes these are agreeable arrangements, as with dogs and cats, or cows and canaries. Other times they are less welcome as with mice and cockroaches which feed in the kitchen, rabbits which chew up the vegetable garden, or raccoons which feed at garbage pails. The animals in this chapter are familiar as themselves or as somehow related to those most of us know in our daily life. • Millenniums ago, after men had developed agriculture and taken up a relatively settled life, they began to make wild animals useful by taming them and keeping them around their settlements. A domestic animal was a source of food always at hand, its flesh available when needed. With the invention of the wheel during the Bronze Age, the ox and horse took on new importance as draught animals. The introduction of the stirrup during the Middle Ages revolutionized both war and peaceful transportation. Horse racing became the sport of royalty and painting horse portraits became a hugely profitable business for artists. One British duke boasted that he paid more for a portrait of his horse than he did for one of his duchess. • Some animals have been domesticated in ways that are limited by climate— reindeer, for example, in northern Europe. An American relative of the reindeer, a predecessor of the beast on page 63, served at the end of the eighteenth century to set European science

FAMILIAR FRIENDS AND NEIGHBORS

straight. At that time, a perverse group of European zoologists, led by the renowned Comte de Buffon, held a low opinion of the animals of the New World. Its birds, they said, were drab and unmelodious while its animals were puny and powerless. To prove them wrong, Jefferson had a huge New Hampshire moose shot, stuffed, and shipped to Buffon who, impressed by the huge American beast, told Jefferson he would take back his slander. • Domestication does not adequately describe what has happened with cats and dogs, which have carried the process to an extreme by becoming family members. Modern cats descend from wild breeds in Egypt. Dogs, the first animals to be domesticated, are all descendants of the wolf. Probably the process began when wolves found that feeding at kitchen middens, early man's rubbish heaps, was easier than chasing down wild prey. As social animals, bonded to a leader, wolves accepted men's presence and man gradually came to value theirs. • Actually the cat, basically a solitary animal, is not classed as domesticated. It has not been that in spirit either. Even the tamest tabby purring in a lap, still keeps the character of Rudyard Kipling's "cat that walks by itself," its innermost self still "in the wild wild woods waving his wild tail." The dog, as opposite as can be, was summed up once and for all by Harriet Beecher Stowe, whose eulogy of the dog as "nothing but organized love, love on four feet that would die for you," still gives dog lovers an acute case of lump in the throat.

20 ▪ DOMESTIC CAT *Felis catus*

"Of the Cat." Woodcut. In *History of four-footed beasts and serpents . . .* by Edward Topsell (1658). ▪ First issued in 1608, Edward Topsell's free translation of portions of Conrad Gesner's landmark zoology *Historiae animalium* was the first important book on animals to be published in English. Topsell, a cleric, not only perpetuated many of the superstitions that Gesner included with his valuable first-hand observations but added fictions of his own. The woodcut illustrations from Gesner account in large part for the book's enduring popularity. Despite their crudity and anatomical errors, such as this cat's tiny ears and odd forehead markings, most of the illustrations capture the spirit of their subjects.

CANIS DINGO, *Blumenb.*

21 · DINGO *Canis familiaris*

"Canis Dingo." Hand-colored lithograph, by John Gould and Henry Constantine Richter. In *The mammals of Australia* by John Gould (1845–63). ▪ Gould noted that Dingos raid sheep pens, wantonly destroying more animals than they eat, and that English settlers nostalgic for the blood sports of their homeland would conduct fox hunts "down under," with a Dingo as the quarry.

Canis jubatus.

22 • MANED WOLF *Chrysocyon brachyurus*

"Canis jubatus." Hand-colored lithograph, by Hermann Burmeister. In *Erläuterungen zur Fauna Brasiliens . . .* by Hermann Burmeister (1856). ▪ In a lavishly illustrated study of Brazilian quadrupeds, Burmeister introduced to European science one of the handsomest members of the dog family. Named for its furry mane, the wolf is distinguished also by a foxlike muzzle, large ears, and elegant long legs, which enable it to travel easily through tall grasses.

Pl. 95.

Fig. 1.ᵉʳᵉ
Le Chat Sauvage.

Fig. 2.
Le Chat domestique.

Fig. 3. Le Chat d'Angora.

Histoire Naturelle, Quadrupèdes.

Benard Direxit
5o.

23 ▪ DOMESTIC CAT *Felis catus*

"Le Chat Sauvage; Le Chat domestique; Le Chat d'Angora." Etching, by Benard from drawing by J. E. DeSève. In *Encyclopédie methodique . . .* (1774–1832), vol. 135: *Mammalogie* by Anselme-Gaetan Desmarest (1820). ▪ The massive *Encyclopédie methodique* is one of the amazing monuments of eighteenth-century French scholarship, similar in many respects to the better known *Encyclopédie* of Dennis Diderot. The mammals were all depicted by DeSève, who arranged them, several to a page, to correspond to Desmarest's text. Shown here is a wild cat (actually a feral domestic cat), a house cat, and an aristocrat of the cat world, a long-haired Angora.

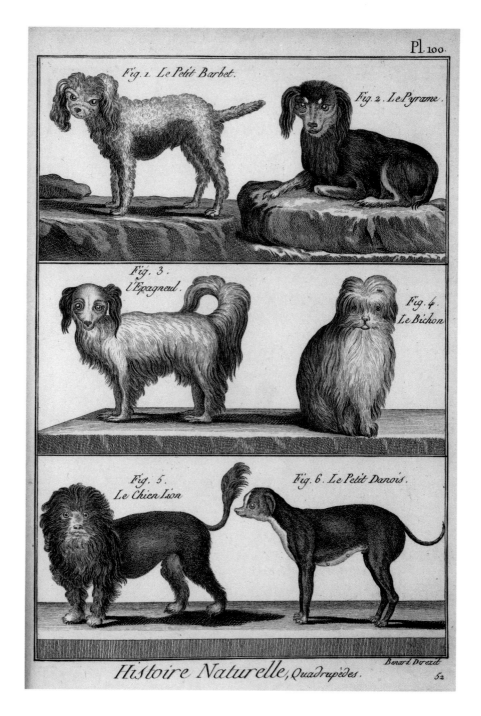

Fig. 1. Le Petit Barbet.

Fig. 2. Le Pyrame.

Fig. 3. L'Epagneul.

Fig. 4. Le Bichon.

Fig. 5. Le Chien Lion.

Fig. 6. Le Petit Danois.

Histoire Naturelle, Quadrupèdes.

Benard Direxit

52

24 ▪ DOMESTIC DOG *Canis familiaris*

"Le Petit Barbet; Le Pyrame; L'Epagneul; Le Bichon; Le Chien Lion; Le Petit Danois." Etching, by Benard from drawing by J. E. DeSève. In *Encyclopédie methodique* . . . (1774–1832), vol. 135: *Mammalogie* by Anselme-Gaetan Desmarest (1820). ▪ Unlike domestic cats, which all resemble a prototype, dogs have been bred into hundreds of varied shapes, colors, and sizes, ranging from the two-pound Chihuahua to the nearly three-hundred pound St. Bernard. The "Little Spaniel," Bichon (now known as Bichon Frise), and the "Lion Dog" (known as Lowchen) are shown here.

Water Dog.

Pub.by W.Darton & J.Harvey. Sept.r 1.st 1808.

25 ▪ DOMESTIC DOG *Canis familiaris*

"Water Dog." Etching, from drawing by Samuel Howitt. In *Memoirs of British quadrupeds . . .* by William Bingley (1809). ▪ Reverend Bingley seems to have had a great deal of time from pastoral duties in view of his enormous output of popular books, which dealt mostly with natural history subjects. In *Memoirs* Bingley describes twenty-two types of dogs. He considered the Water Dog to be of Spanish descent. In his chatty text Bingley tells of a Water Dog whose curly hair "is so soft and fine in its texture, that the owner cuts it off twice in the year, and each fleece is found sufficient to be manufactured into two hats."

London. Pub. as the Act directs by E. Donovan & F. C & J. Rivingtons August 1 1818.

26 ▪ DOMESTIC DOG *Canis familiaris*

"Fox-hound." Hand-colored etching, by Edward Donovan from his own drawing. In *The Natural History of British Quadrupeds . . .* by Edward Donovan (1820). ▪ Today there are over four hundred recognized dog breeds. The Foxhound is the dog usually associated with the old and still extant sport of fox-hunting. It is distinguished for qualities that make it useful to the chase: stamina, speed, a keen nose, and a courageous yet obedient nature.

TEES-WATER IMPROVED BREED.

By persevering in the same laudable plan of improvement so successfully begun by the late Mr Bakewell, the stock-farmers or graziers of Tees-water have produced a kind which is looked upon by judges as nearly approaching to perfection. Many of their Sheep possess the thriving or fattening quality of the Dishley breed, and are fit for the butcher at as early an age.

These Sheep weigh from twenty-five to forty-five pounds per quarter; some have been fed to fifty pounds; and one in particular was killed, which weighed sixty-two pounds ten ounces per quarter, avoirdupoise; a circumstance never before heard of in this island. The Ewes of this breed generally bring forth two Lambs each season: sometimes three, four,

27 ▪ DOMESTIC SHEEP *Ovis aries*

"Tees-Water Improved Breed." Wood-engraving, by Thomas Bewick. In *A general history of quadrupeds* by Thomas Bewick (1824). ▪ Among the finest representations of familiar animals are the tiny, lively, and amazingly detailed illustrations of Thomas Bewick, the British naturalist, artist, and printmaker, whose technical innovations renewed the old craft of wood-block printing. The "improvements" made to this sheep would seem for the benefit of the farmer. "It is now fit for the butcher at an earlier age," wrote Bewick.

THE OLD LINCOLN BREED.
Ram, bred by Mr Jex, St Jecmains, near Lynne, County of Norfolk.
PROFESSOR LOW'S ILLUSTRATIONS OF THE BREEDS OF THE DOMESTIC ANIMALS
Published June, 1841, by Longmans, Orme, Brown, Green & Longmans, Paternoster Row, London.

28 ▪ DOMESTIC SHEEP *Ovis aries*

"The Old Lincoln Breed." Hand-colored lithograph, by Fairland from drawing by W. Nicholson after painting by William Shiels. In *The Breeds of the domestic animals of the British Islands . . .* by David Low (1842). ▪ There are over eight hundred breeds of domestic sheep, raised for their meat, milk, and wool. The fleece of the Lincoln type is the longest, densest, and heaviest of all the British breeds. Low noted that this corpulent ram yielded ten to twelve pounds of wool annually, and also that the breed, in its pure form, was nearing extinction.

25

London Pub. as the Act directs by E.Donovan & F.C.J.Rivingtons June 1.1819.

29 ▪ DOMESTIC CATTLE *Bos taurus*

"Tame or Domesticated Ox." Hand-colored etching, from his own drawing by Edward Donovan. In *The Natural History of British Quadrupeds . . .* by Edward Donovan (1820). ▪ This miniature scene is typical of the delicately rendered and finely colored natural history plates that the industrious Edward Donovan produced. Best known for his ten-volume *Natural History of British Birds* (1794–1819), Donovan also wrote, illustrated, etched the plates, and often hand-colored the prints of a series of small-format books devoted to the insects, molluscs, fish, and quadrupeds of Great Britain, as well as the insects of China and India.

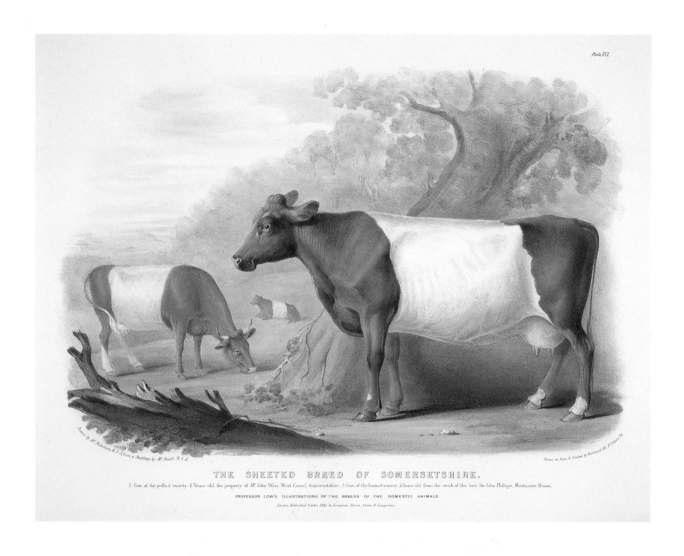

30 ▪ DOMESTIC CATTLE *Bos taurus*

"The Sheeted Breed of Somersetshire." Hand-colored lithograph, by Fairland from drawing by W. Nicholson, after painting by William Shiels. In *The Breeds of the domestic animals of the British Islands . . .* by David Low (1842). ▪ Shown are two four-year-old varieties of the cow of this now extinct breed, one horned, the other polled, or hornless. They were exemplary domestic cattle: both hardy and docile, the cows were good milkers and the steers produced fine beef.

Pl. 1. LE SARIGUE *Mâle.* T. 28. S. 5.

LE SARIGUE *femelle.*

Demanchy *S.*

31 ▪ BROWN FOUR-EYED OPOSSUM *Metachirus nudicaudatus*

"Le Sarigue, mâle . . . femelle." Etching, by Demanchy from drawing by J. E. DeSève or Jacques Barraband. In *Histoire naturelle . . .* by Le Comte de Buffon (1799–1808). ▪ George Louis LeClercq, Le Comte de Buffon, was Superintendent for half a century of the Royal Gardens in Paris, and based his exhaustive, multivolume "Natural History" on its extensive collections. His detailed descriptions of hundreds of animals achieved immediate popularity; more than fifty French editions, numerous translations, and hundreds of abridgments of his work appeared and influenced science into the nineteenth century.

Didelphys palmata.
½ nat. Gr.

32 ▪ WATER OPOSSUM *Chironectes minimus*

"Didelphys palmatal." Hand-colored lithograph, by Hermann Burmeister. In *Erläuterungen zur Fauna Brasiliens . . .* by Hermann Burmeister (1856). ▪ This strange marsupial, also called the Yapok, is a relative of the Common, or Virginia, Opossum but unlike other New World opossums it is at home in the water. Its fur is waterproof, it can seal its ears, its hind feet are webbed, and the female's pouch entraps air for her tiny infants during underwater dives. When they outgrow this bathyspheric chamber the young travel with the mother in the water by clinging to the fur on her back. Burmeister travelled extensively in Brazil, Argentina, and Mexico, describing the geography as well as the natural history of these lands in his many books.

33 ▪ 1. NORTHERN BIRCH MOUSE *Sicista betulina* ▪ 2. SOUTHERN BIRCH MOUSE *S. subtilis*

"Mus Betulinus; Mus Vagus." Etching in two states, hand-colored and uncolored, by I. Nussbiegel from drawing by Nitschmann. In *Novae species quadrupedum . . .* by Peter Simon Pallas (1778–79). ▪ The natural sciences in eighteenth and early nineteenth century Russia were immeasurably enriched by the contributions of Peter Simon Pallas, a German-born field researcher and writer who devoted much of his long career to the zoology, botany, and geology of that vast country and its surrounding regions. Artistic license is evident in this joint portrait of birch mice from Scandinavia and northern Europe since the two species actually favor different habitats.

Igelkott.
(*Erinaceus europaeus.* Linn.)

34 ▪ HEDGEHOG *Erinaceus europaeus*

"Igelkott." Hand-colored lithograph, by Magnus Köerner. In *Illuminerade Figurer till Skandinaviens Fauna . . .* by Sven Nilsson (1832–40). ▪ Despite a formidable protective shield of several thousand sharp quills, this familiar Old World insectivore is sometimes kept as an unusual—and distinctly un-cuddly—pet. Hedgehogs also appear in two beloved classics of English children's literature. Mrs. Tiggy-Winkle is one of Beatrix Potter's enduring animal characters, and the animal's protective behavior of curling into a tight ball was adapted in Lewis Carroll's *Alice in Wonderland*—there the sphere-like hedgehog was made into a croquet ball for the Queen of Heart's croquet game.

35 ▪ EUROPEAN HARE *Lepus capensis* ▪ SNOW HARE *L. timidus*
  ▪ IMAGINARY HARE ▪ HYBRID(?) HARE *L. sp.*

"1. Le Lièvre; 2. L. variable; 3. L. cornu; 4. L. Métis." Etching, by Benard from drawing by J. E. DeSève. In *Encyclopédie methodique . . .* (1774–1832), vol. 135: *Mammalogie* by Anselme-Gaetan Desmarest (1820). ▪ Depicted with three real animals is the notorious horned or antlered hare. Taxidermists seem to have had a particular fondness for attaching horns or antlers (depending on what was locally available) to ordinary hares.

36 • EUROPEAN HARE *Lepus capensis* • IMAGINARY HORNED HARE

"Der Hase." Hand-colored etching from drawing, by Gottlieb Tobias Wilhelm. In *Unterhaltungen aus der Naturgeschichte . . .* by Gottlieb Tobias Wilhelm (1792–1802). • There are distinct differences between hares and rabbits. Hares have longer legs and ears, are generally solitary, do not burrow, and bear fully furred, open-eyed young who can hop about almost immediately. Rabbits burrow together sociably and their kits are born blind, bald, and helpless.

Plate 2.

SIAMESE BREED.

Sow, 3 Years old, imported from Singapore by Mess.ʳˢ Dudgale, Manchester:. The litter by a half-bred Chinese Male.

Published June, 1840, by Longman, Orme, Brown, Green & Longmans, Paternoster Row, London.

37 ▪ DOMESTIC PIG *Sus scrofa*

"Siamese Breed." Hand-colored lithograph, by Fairland from drawing by W. Nicholson after painting by William Shiels. In *The Breeds of the domestic animals of the British Islands . . .* by David Low (1842). ▪ These multicolor piglets resulted from the union of this three-year-old sow from Singapore and a "half-bred Chinese Male." The so-called Siamese breed, small pigs whose bellies just clear the ground because of their short legs, may be ancestors of the miniature "Chinese" or "Vietnamese Potbellied Pigs."

OLD ENGLISH BREED.

Old English Sow, from the midland Counties.

Published June, 1840, by Longmans Orme Brown, Green, & Longmans, Paternoster Row London.

38 ▪ DOMESTIC PIG *Sus scrofa*

"Old English Breed." Hand-colored lithograph, by Fairland from drawing by W. Nicholson after painting by William Shiels. In *The Breeds of the domestic animals of the British Islands . . .* by David Low (1842). ▪ The history, breeding, care, diseases, and economic value of over fifty breeds of domestic animals are discussed in this lavishly illustrated work. Low, who also wrote several breeders' manuals, was Professor of Agriculture at the University of Edinburgh. His comments on this bicolored sow included his observation that Americans consumed more pork than any other people.

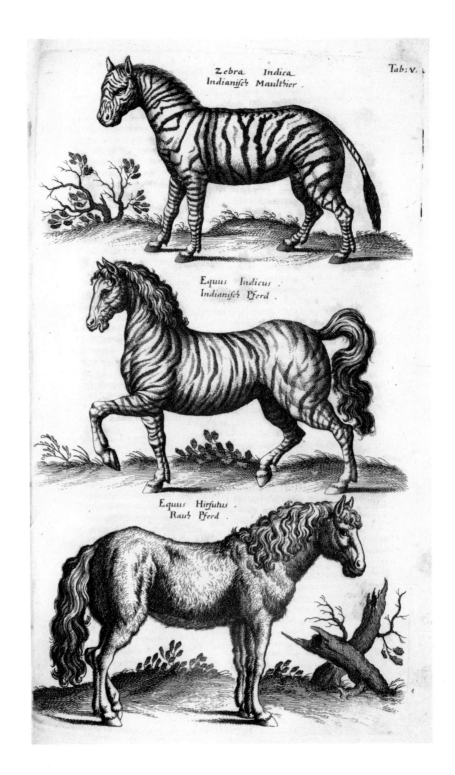

39 ▪ BURCHELL'S ZEBRA *Equus burchelli* ▪ DOMESTIC HORSE *E. caballus*

"Zebra Indica; Equus Indicus; Equus Hirsutus." Engraving, by Matthaeus Merian the Younger from his own drawing. In *Historia naturalis de quadrupedibus . . .* by John Jonston (1655). ▪ Although Jonston's "Natural History" was a popular book, it promulgated any number of "imaginative" errors. In this case, he has written that Burchell's zebra comes from India, even though no zebras occur in that region.

Devise.
La Bride est ma Vertu.

Pl. 1.

Favori, un Barbe de Tunis.

40 ▪ DOMESTIC HORSE *Equus caballus*

"Favori, un Barbe de Tunis." Engraving, by Bernard Picart [?] from drawing by Baron Reis d'Eisenberg. In *L'anti-maquignonage pour éviter la surprise dans l'emplette des chevaux* by Baron Reis d'Eisenberg (1764). ▪ This manual instructs buyers how to "avoid surprises when purchasing a horse" and is replete with descriptions and illustrations of the various desirable and less-than-desirable features. Barb and Arabian horses were progenitors of the modern racehorse. Favori, considered by the Baron a fine example of his breed, is portrayed with the heraldic banner, "My Bridle is My Device."

Shetland Pony. Forester. Welch Pony.

Painted by Benj.ⁿ Marshall. Engraved by John Scott.

PONIES.

To JACOB WARDELL, ESQ.^R this Plate is Respectfully Inscribed by the PROPRIETORS.

Published Novr 1. 1809. by James Candee & John Jott. London.

41 ▪ DOMESTIC HORSE *Equus caballus*

"Ponies." Engraving, with etching and aquatint by John Scott from painting by Benjamin Marshall. In *History and delineation of the horse . . .* by John Lawrence (1809). ▪ The breeding, care, diseases, and general management of all types of horses is discussed by Lawrence, although his focus is on racehorses. Included among the finely executed engravings, all of which derive from paintings by leading artists of this genre, are portraits of several great racers.

THE OLD ENGLISH BLACK HORSE.
Stallion, by old Blacklegs, from a Mare of the Dishley breed ... bred by Mr Brownes, at Ormiston, Derby.
PROFESSOR LOW'S ILLUSTRATIONS OF THE BREEDS OF THE DOMESTIC ANIMALS

42 • DOMESTIC HORSE *Equus caballus*

"The Old English Black Horse." Hand-colored lithograph, by Fairland from drawing by W. Nicholson after painting by William Shiels. In *The Breeds of the domestic animals of the British Islands . . .* by David Low (1842). ▪ Lithographs of paintings by the Scottish artist William Shiels in the Agricultural Museum of the University of Edinburgh illustrate David Low's classic study. This stallion "by Old Blacklegs, from a Mare of the Dishley Blood," is a handsome example of the heavy and powerful but slow breed used for field work, and to pull carriages and brewery and coal wagons.

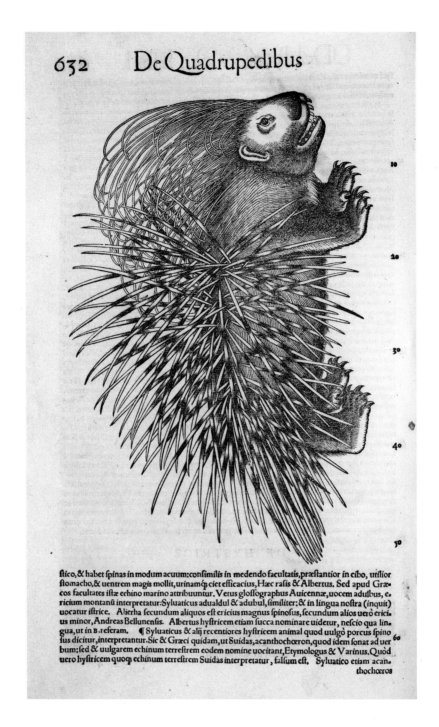

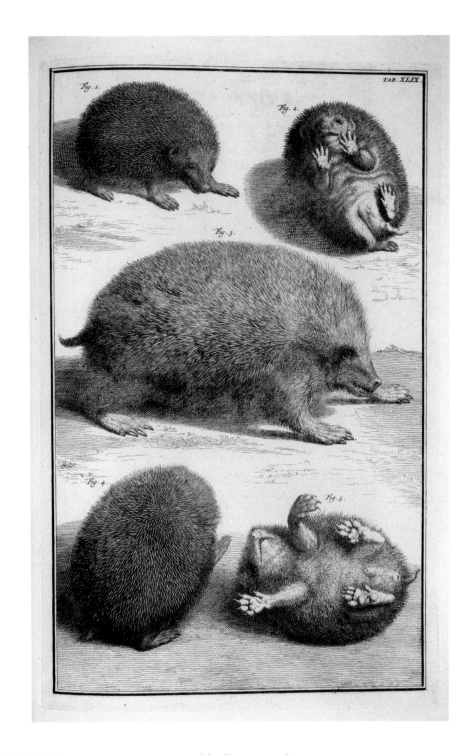

44 · HEDGEHOG *Erinaceus europaeus*, possibly *E. amurensis*

"1,2. Petit Herrisson, de nôtre Païs; 3. H. d'Amerique . . . ; 4,5. H. de Siberie. . . ." Engraving. In *Locupletissimi rerum naturalium thesauri . . .* by Albert Seba (1734–65). ▪ Seba had many collaborators in the compilation of the enormous catalogue of his natural history collections. The great classifier, Linnaeus, was also invited to participate but declined. When *Locupletissimi* was completed, however, Linnaeus used many of the well-drawn figures as references in his taxonomic classic, *Systema naturae*.

45 ▪ COMMON GIANT FLYING SQUIRREL *Petaurista petaurista*

"Brilliant Flying Squirrel." Hand-colored lithograph, by Benjamin Waterhouse Hawkins. In *Illustrations of Indian Zoology . . .* by John Edward Gray and Thomas Hardwicke (1830–34). ▪ The illustrations of this rare study of the native vertebrate fauna are based largely on the specimens and drawings collected by Major-General Hardwicke during his forty years of service in India. The many species of so-called flying squirrels travel, sometimes for considerable distances, from tree to tree by gliding, supported by the patagium, the membrane stretched between the fore and hind limbs. Their whiskered tail serves as a rudder.

PETAURISTA TAGUANOÏDES.

46 ▪ GREATER GLIDING POSSUM *Schoinobates volans*

"Petaurista Taguanoïdes." Hand-colored lithograph, by John Gould and Henry Constantine Richter. In *The mammals of Australia* by John Gould (1845–63). ▪ Possums should not be confused with opossums. The New World opossums are one of the few marsupial groups found outside of Australia, while possums or phalangers are one of many Australian pouched mammals. The nocturnal, cat-sized Greater Glider is found in New South Wales. Like the flying squirrels it glides from tree to tree, kept aloft by the gliding membrane, which also serves as a blanket in cold weather. Like its close relative, the koala, the Greater Glider feeds largely on eucalyptus foliage.

INDIAN ZIBETH. VIVERRA ZIBETTA. Linn.
Viverra Undulata. Gray.

Drawn on Stone by Waterhouse Hawkins from the living Specimen in the Surry Zoological Gardens.

47 ▪ LARGE SPOTTED CIVET *Viverra megaspila*

"Indian Zibeth—Viverra Zibetta." Hand-colored lithograph, by Benjamin Waterhouse Hawkins. In *Illustrations of Indian Zoology . . .* by John Edward Gray and Thomas Hardwicke (1830–34). ▪ The Viverridae family includes mongooses, genets, and civets, many boldly patterned, such as the live model that Waterhouse Hawkins depicted, which was misidentified as an Indian Civet, or Zibeth.

A PRAIRIE DOG TOWN.

48 ▪ PRAIRIE DOG *Cynomys ludovicianus*

"A Prairie Dog Town." Wood-engraving, by G. Pearson from drawing by F. W. Keyl or E. Smith. In *Homes without hands . . .* by John George Wood (1866). ▪ Reverend John Wood was a compulsive, prolific author, whose numerous natural histories were once very popular, but are remembered now for their fine illustrations but dull texts. Black-tailed Prairie Dogs are large, sociable rodents of the western United States. These master architects burrow underground towns which extend for hundreds of square miles, housing hundreds of thousands of residents.

PTEROPUS POLIOCEPHALUS, *1/anim.*

49 ▪ GREY-HEADED FLYING FOX *Pteropus poliocephalus*

"Pteropus Poliocephalus." Hand-colored lithograph, by John Gould and Henry Constantine Richter. In *The mammals of Australia* by John Gould (1845–63). ▪ This bat was known as the "Grey-headed Vampire" in the nineteenth century, a misnomer since it eats fruit and, like most bats, never drinks blood. Named for their vulpine muzzles, the flying foxes are the largest and probably the most attractive of the bats, a group relentlessly persecuted by fearful, misinformed humans. With the exception of the parasitic vampires, who also transmit diseases, bats are not only harmless but extremely beneficial to mankind: the fruit eaters, despite their depredations of orchards, are vital pollinators and seed dispersers.

Plate LXI

On Stone by W. H. Hitchcock

Raccoon.

Drawn from Nature by J.W. Audubon.

Lith. Printed & Col.ᵈ by J.T. Bowen, Phil.

50 ▪ RACCOON *Procyon lotor*

"Raccoon." Hand-colored lithograph, by William E. Hitchcock from drawing by John Woodhouse Audubon. In *The quadrupeds of North America* by John James Audubon and John Bachman (1849–54). ▪ Just as the illustration captures the spirit of one of North America's most familiar wild animals, so the text zeroes in on its habits, especially one that makes this otherwise attractive creature anathema to gardeners—its ability to divine exactly when corn is about to ripen. This nimble night raider can devastate an entire corn patch just hours before its rightful owner had planned his own harvest.

Paralipomena.   1099

CAPRICORNI uel potius ibicis maris figura, quam similiter
cum eius historia angustiorem posueramus.
Steinbock.

51 ▪ IBEX *Capra ibex*

"Capricorni." Woodcut. In *Historiae animalium . . .* by Conrad Gesner (1551–87). ▪ In his masterpiece, considered the starting point of modern zoology, Gesner attempted to compile everything then known about animals. The Zurich-born naturalist, physician, and bibliographer augmented the findings (and in the case of fabulous beasts, the folly) of the past with his own observations. The excellent, anonymous illustrations were woodcuts prepared in the workshop of Gesner's publisher, Christopher Froschauer. Many derive from earlier published works by Guillaume Rondelet, Olaus Magnus, Pierre Bélon, and Ippolito Salviani.

THE ELK.
JARDIN DU ROI

London. Published Aug.1 1832 by Moon, Boys & Graves, Printsellers to the King. 6 Pall Mall.

52 ▪ MOOSE *Alces alces*

"The Elk." Etching, by Thomas Landseer from his own drawing. In *Characteristic sketches of animals . . .* by John Henry Barrow (1832). ▪ Most of Landseer's subjects were residents of British zoos. This Moose, however, hailed from Paris's Jardin des Plantes. *A. alces* is called an elk everywhere but in the United States, although Barrow recognized that his subject was the same animal as the "American Moose Deer."

EAST CAUCASIAN TUR.

Published by Rowland Ward, Ltd.

53 ▪ EAST CAUCASIAN TUR *Capra aegagrus*

"East Caucasian Tur." Chromolithograph, by Josef Wolf. In *Wild oxen, sheep, and goats . . .* by Richard Lydekker (1898). ▪ Josef Wolf's portrait of these wild goats is typical of the vigor and sense of movement he brought to all his animal subjects, although he is equally well known for his bird portraits for the numerous ornithologies of John Gould. He spent innumerable hours observing and sketching living animals, in zoos and in the wild, and even when he worked with specimens, his knowledge of the living animal was conveyed through his art. Although the magnificently horned Tur is a prized game animal, Wolf was interested only in capturing it on paper—he had no use for blood "sports."

EUROPEAN MUFLON.

Published by Rowland Ward Ltd.

54 ▪ EUROPEAN MUFLON *Ovis musimon*

"European Muflon." Chromolithograph, by Josef Wolf. In *Wild oxen, sheep, and goats . . .* by Richard Lydekker (1898). ▪ These wild ancestors of domestic sheep are extremely hardy and nimble-footed, inhabiting inhospitable cold and dry desert areas and mountain peaks in Asia Minor, Europe, Corsica, Sardinia, and Cyprus. The impressive horns are borne only by the rams; the ewes are either hornless, or occasionally bear tiny horns. Lydekker, who edited the extremely popular multivolume *Royal Natural History*, which was illustrated with hundreds of lively wood engravings, was an authority on game animals. *Wild oxen . . .* is part of his larger work, *Game mammals of the world.*

Birds have always been, in Cole Porter's words, "so easy to love" that people hardly ever stop to consider why they do love birds more easily than any other family of animals. Because birds are so beautiful, they say, or because birds seem so free, or because their songs are so sweet or their habits so interesting. Or because they bring out the poetry in nature. Actually, what birds do is bring out the poet in the most unpoetical of people. Few men in history have been more hard-headed than Cardinal Barbarini, the sixteenth-century churchman who, as Pope Urban VII, harshly condemned Galileo for his heretical theories. But when Ulysses Aldrovandi showed the Cardinal the illustrations for his *Ornithology* back around 1600, the Cardinal went into raptures over what he called "The winged inhabitants of the air." Aldrovandi, a scientist at the University of Bologna, set an example for future ornithologists by going out on organized bird walks to study his subject in the field, taking artists along so they could make accurate renderings to explain and enliven his 2,600 pages of text. ▪ Mixed in with all their affections for birds is people's feeling that, more than any other creatures, birds need special protection. The Bible, which scorns dogs and never once mentions cats, says that "The sparrow has found a house and the swallow a nest in the house of the Lord." Protecting birds became a matter of morality. St. Francis in his touching sermon to the birds told them that "whereas you neither sow nor reap He himself doth protect you without any care of your own" and the birds, responding, "showed by their songs their joy." And well they might sing for Francis was promoting the fallacy that birds are helpless and carefree creatures. ▪ The notion, however saintly, that birds are frail creatures of irreproachable character and fair intentions goes against all the evidence. Birds are rough, adversarial, selfish, and well able to take care of themselves. Tiny wrens raid other bird's nests, pecking holes in eggs and in baby birds' heads. Crows eat young robins and song sparrows of both sexes make off with other sparrows' mates. This of course is no worse than the behavior of all animals governed by the need to survive in an unforgiving world. ▪ If birds have reason to appreciate men for protecting them, men can appreciate birds for showing them the need to preserve nature. The first organized conservation movements began in the middle of the nineteenth century with men who first joined together for the pleasures of watching birds and later took on the duty of preserving them. After a while, these men came to speak not just for birds but for all nature. Out of their activities came the first international conservation laws and the methods of bird protection groups became models for the environmental movement. Birds are the most visible signs of what happens to nature when fragile environments are exploited. ▪ They demonstrate the enormous interdependence of nature, of the need to leave nature alone so that it can keep its own balance. In the end, self-interest has confirmed what morality first taught.

WINGED INHABITANTS OF THE AIR

DE STRVTHOCAMELO.

A.

S TRVTHOCAMELVS nomen Græcum eft, quod etiam Latini receperunt, Plinius
& alij: etſi quidam ſtruthiocamelum ſex ſyllabis ſcribant, quod non probo. Recentiores
Latini ſtruthionem dicunt, ut Hieronymus & eo poſteriores: (apud Iul. Capitolinũ ſtru-
thiones Mauros legimus: ſexcentorum ſtruthionum apud Lampridiũ) quos etiam docti
quidam imitantur, Gaza & alij. Et quoniam Græci σρυθὸγ μεγάλω uel λιϐυκω̃, hanc auem uocant,
plerunꝗ fœminino genere (Ariſtoteles tamẽ σρουθὸς ὁ ὂν λιϐύη, maſc. gen. Gaza ſtruthionem Africam
dixit, & alibi ſtruthionem Libycum,) recentiorum quoꝗ nõnulli fœm. gen. ſtruthionem magnam
uel Li-

55 ▪ OSTRICH *Struthio camelus*

"De Struthocamelo." Woodcut. In *Historiae animalium . . .* by Conrad Gesner (1551–87). ▪ The flightless ostriches are the largest living birds and now occur in the wild only on the plains of Africa. They are swift runners, and defend themselves with their powerful legs, kicking and slashing at attackers. Although Gesner has shown the lively demeanor for which these birds are noted, he has drawn the plumage incorrectly.

Drawn from Nature by A. Wilson.   1. Long-tailed Duck.   2. Female.   3. Summer D.   4. Green-winged Teal.   5. Canvas-back D.   6. Red-headed D.   7. Mallard.   Engraved by A. Lawson.
70

56 ▪ SEVEN DUCKS sub-family *Anatinae*

Hand-colored engraving, with etching, by Alexander Lawson from drawing by Alexander Wilson. In *American ornithology . . .* by Alexander Wilson (1808–14). ▪ Although it is possible that the waterfowl depicted by Wilson would share the same habitat, it is unlikely. The Oldsquaw, *Clangula hyemalis* (1. male; 2. female), also called the Long Tailed Duck, breeds in the arctic tundra and winters along the seacoasts. The tree-perching Wood Duck, *Aix sponsa*(3), previously the Summer Duck, the Green-winged Teal, *Anas crecca*(4), and the Mallard, *A. platyrhynchos*(7) are all freshwater ducks, while the divers—the Canvasback, *Aythya valisineria*(5), and Redhead, *A. americana*(6)—nest near fresh water and winter in bays.

57 ▪ WOOD STORK *Mycteria americana* ▪ SCARLET IBIS *Eudocimus ruber* ▪
GREATER FLAMINGO *Phoenicopterus ruber* ▪ WHITE IBIS *E. albus*

"Wood Ibis; Scarlet Ibis; Flamingo; White Ibis." Hand-colored engraving, with etching, by J. G. Warnicke from
drawing by Alexander Wilson. In *American ornithology . . .* by Alexander Wilson (1808–14). ▪ Wilson is known as
the "Father of American Ornithology," a title he shares both with the eighteenth-century artist Mark Catesby and his
own flamboyant contemporary, John James Audubon. Wilson's classic work was both the first great American
ornithology and the first color-plate book of top rank on any subject published in the United States. Wilson grouped
birds of the same type together, usually without any background. These four long-legged waders have been put
together in an appropriate shore setting.

EGRET.

Designed & Engraved by Will.ᵐ Daniell & Published by Meʃ.ᵗ Cadell & Davies London May 1 1812.

58 ▪ LITTLE EGRET *Egretta garzetta*

"Egret." Monochrome aquatint, by William Daniell from his own drawing. In *Interesting selections from animated nature . . .* by William Daniell (1809). ▪ The aquatint medium, which simulates the soft tones and subtle colors of watercolor painting, was often used to illustrate atlases containing scenic views, but only rarely for the depiction of animal subjects. The Little Egret, similar to the Snowy Egret of the New World, is also adorned with long, slender head plumes. Daniell, whose observations of an animal nearly always stressed its relationship or usefulness to people, wrote admiringly of the egret's beautiful plumage as an adornment in turbans, helmets, and ladies' headdresses.

STRUTHIO CAMELUS (Femina)   L'AUTRUCHE FEMELE.

59 ▪ OSTRICH *Struthio camelus*

"L'Autruche femele." Etching, by Simon Miger from painting by Nicolas Maréchal. In *La Ménagerie du Muséum National d'Histoire Naturelle* by Nicolas Maréchal (1801). ▪ Text authors Count Lacépède and Baron Cuvier considered this illustration the best yet published of an ostrich. Not only did they discuss in great detail each animal's anatomy, habits, and history, they evaluated all previously published illustrations.

T. 13.
Sturnus niger alis supernis rubro colore.
The red Wing'd Starling.
Myrtus Brabanticæ Similis Caroliniensis humilior; foliis latioribus, et magis Serratis.
The broad leaved candle-berry Myrtle.

60 ▪ RED-WINGED BLACKBIRD *Agelaius phoeniceus*

"The red Wing'd Starling." Hand-colored etching, by Mark Catesby from his own drawing. In *The Natural History of Carolina, Florida and the Bahama Islands* . . . by Mark Catesby (2d ed., 1754). ▪ His wings outstretched to show off his distinctive red and gold epaulets, the sprightly male Red-wing is perched on the "Broad Leaved Candle-berry Myrtle," now the Broad-leaved Bayberry. Catesby's integration of native plants with his animal portraits is a reminder that his original mission in the New World was botanical, the collection of American plants and seeds. Red-wings are among the earliest songbirds to return to their northern breeding grounds, the males arriving several weeks ahead of the females to establish their territories.

61 ▪ CHANNEL-BILLED TOUCAN *Ramphastos vitellinus ariel* ▪ RED-BREASTED TOUCAN *R. dicolorus*

"1. Ramphastos Ariel. 2. Ramphastos Discolorus." Chromolithograph, by Waterlow and Sons from drawing by Jean T. Descourtilz. In *Ornithologie brésilienne* by Jean T. Descourtilz (1852, 1854–56). ▪ These lively toucans are typical of the hand of Descourtilz—colorful, vigorously depicted birds artfully set among their food plants. Descourtilz' valuable investigations of Brazilian ornithology and botany were sponsored by the National Museum in Rio de Janeiro. He died in 1855, three years after the publication of *Ornithologie brésilienne*, poisoned while experimenting with native medicines for birds.

Der gehäubte Steissfuss — Weibchen.

Podiceps cristatus — Lath:

Susemihl junxpinx

Susemihl fecit

62 ▪ GREAT CRESTED GREBE _Podiceps cristatus_

"Der gehäubte Steissfuss—Weibchen." Hand-colored etching, by Johann Conrad Susemihl from drawing by Edouard Susemihl. In _Teutsche Ornithologie . . ._ by Moritz B. Borkhausen and others (1800–17). ▪ _Teutsche Ornithologie_ is the German counterpart to other lavish national ornithologies, especially the works of the Frenchman François Levaillant. The drawing, engraving, printing, and coloring of its 132 plates were mostly a Susemihl family project involving Johann Conrad Susemihl, his son Edouard, and his brother, Johann Theodor. _Podiceps cristatus_ is one of the largest of the grebes and ranges in the Eastern Hemisphere.

Der gemeine Eisvogel — Alcedo ispida — Linn:
1. Mannchen. 2. Weibchen.

63 · EUROPEAN KINGFISHER *Alcedo atthis ispida*

"Der gemeine Eisvogel. 1. Mannchen. 2. Weibchen." Hand-colored etching, by Johann Conrad Susemihl from drawing by Edouard Susemihl. In *Teutsche Ornithologie . . .* by Moritz B. Borkhausen and others (1800–17). ▪ One of several folktales associated with these birds pertains specifically to the European Kingfisher. Originally drab gray in color, it was one of Noah's passengers on the Ark. But late one afternoon it flew westward, and the rays of the setting sun burned its breast reddish brown, while its back assumed the blue-green color of the evening sky.

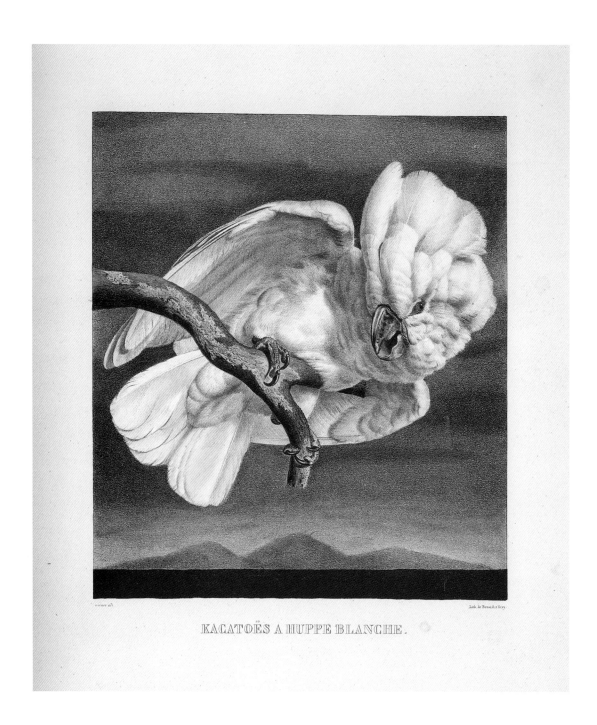

KACATOËS A HUPPE BLANCHE.

64 ▪ WHITE COCKATOO *Cacatua alba*

"Kacatoës a huppe Blanche." Hand-colored lithograph, by Benard from drawing by J. C. Werner. In *Histoire naturelle des perroquets* by Alexandre Bourjot Saint-Hilaire (1837–38). ▪ Set against a dramatic night sky this angry cockatoo, crest raised in excitement, crouches on its perch. Because this parrot was often agitated during its captivity, Florent Prévost, chief taxidermist of the Zoological Laboratories of the Paris Museum, decided to mount it in this state after its demise. Bourjot Saint-Hilaire's beautifully illustrated monograph is intended as a supplement to François Levaillant's two-volume study of the same title of 1801–05.

STRIX FLAMMEA.

65 • BARN OWL *Tyto alba*

"Strix Flammea." Hand-colored engraving, with etching, by C. Sepp or J. C. Sepp from his own drawing. In *Nederlandsche vogelen . . .* by Cornelius Nozeman, Martinus Houttuyn, and Jan Christian Sepp (1770–1829). • The first comprehensive account of all the birds known in the Netherlands is still considered the most beautiful book about that area. It was ahead of its time in its depictions of birds in lifelike attitudes, often in natural settings. The familiar Barn Owl, distributed worldwide, is readily recognized by its long legs, underparts with dark spots, and heart-shaped facial disk. This last, most obvious distinguishing feature has been rendered incorrectly in this otherwise accurate illustration.

When Dr. Thomas Muffet (sometimes spelled Mouffett) proposed around 1590 to write a book on insects, his friends discouraged him. "The study of insects lacked dignity, decency and value," they told him, warning that he "should lose time, charge and labor exceedingly." This was a pervading attitude toward insects. Even the Comte de Buffon, who ruled over European natural history a century later, decreed that "a bee should not occupy more in the head of a naturalist than it does in nature." When a landmark work on entomology, the study of insects, was published early in the nineteenth century, the authors felt they had to go out of their way to defend their subject. "Insects appear to have been nature's favorite productions," they wrote, "in which she has confined and concentrated almost all that is either beautiful or graceful, interesting and alluring, or curious and singular...."
▪ Today with a sense of triumph, entomologists boast that there are more species of insects—creeping up close to a million—than of all other animals combined. Their variety is astonishing—300,000 species of beetles, 112,000 of butterflies and moths. ▪ It wasn't that insects were altogether ignored. In the Old Testament, Isaiah warned that his adversaries "will wear out like a garment; the moth will eat them up." A thirteenth-century ecclesiast named Bartholomew, perhaps slyly mocking his brethren who saw a purpose in all creatures, saw virtue in vermin for provoking man "to recognize his own infirmity and invoke the name of God." ▪ Artists found beauty and a kind of wonder in the microscopic complexities of a beetle's claw and the weird coloration of leaf beetles. The lepidoptera, moths and butterflies, have provided the richest subjects. ▪ The first artist to study both the beauty and nature of butterflies was Maria Sibylla Merian who picked herself up out of a comfortable life in Switzerland in 1685, divorced her husband, and went off to Surinam in South America, enduring a monstrously rough voyage and a rudimentary life to complete the first true study of the process of metamorphosis and to paint, with delicate realism, the insects of her vivid new world. ▪ Thomas Muffet—to get back to that stubborn Elizabethan—was also tough minded. Sighing over "the difficulty of the work . . . Insects are hard to be explained," he went on to complete *The Theatre of Insects.* Muffet admired his subjects very much. Look to the ant, he said, for prudence and to the bee for temperance. "Musician," he instructed, "hearken to the grasshopper." He praised the spider for having "so excellent a temper." ▪ He did not know then that spiders are not really insects, nor could he know that one of them would give his name an immortality that his own work never gained. This was, of course, the sociable spider that came upon a young English miss as she was eating her curds and whey and, sitting down on a tuft of grass beside her, frightened Dr. Muffet's daughter away.

CREEPERS, CRAWLERS AND JEWELED FLIERS

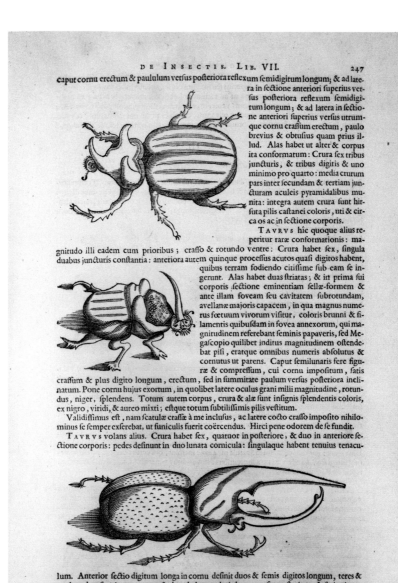

caput cornu erectum & paululum versus posteriora reflexum semidigitum longum; & ad late-ra in sectione anteriori superius ver-sus posteriora reflexum semidigi-tum longum; & ad latera in sectio-ne anteriori superius versus utrum-que cornu crassum erectum, paulo brevius & obtusius quam prius il-lud. Alas habet ut alter & corpus ita conformatum: Crura sex tribus juncturis, & tribus digitis & uno minimo pro quarto: media crurum pars inter secundam & tertiam jun-cturam aculeis pyramidalibus mu-nita: integra autem crura sunt hir-suta pilis castanei coloris, uti & cir-ca os ac in sectione corporis.

TAVRVS hic quoque alius re-peritur rarae conformationis: ma-gnitudo illi eadem cum prioribus; crasso & rotundo ventre: Crura habet sex, singula duabus juncturis constantia: anteriora autem quinque processus acutos quasi digitos habent, quibus terram fodiendo citissime sub eam se in-gerunt. Alas habet duas striatas; & in prima sui corporis sectione eminentiam sellae-formem & ante illam foveam seu cavitatem subrotundam, avellanae majoris capacem, in qua magnus nume-rus foetuum vivorum visitur, coloris brunni & fi-lamentis quibusdam in fovea annexorum, qui ma-gnitudinem referebant seminis papaveris, sed Me-gascopio quilibet indirus magnitudinem ostende-bat pisi, eratque omnibus numeris absolutus & cornutus ut parens. Caput semilunaris fere figu-rae & compressum, cui cornu impositum, satis crassum & plus digito longum, erectum, sed in summitate paulum versus posteriora incli-natum. Pone cornu hujus exortum, in quolibet latere oculus grani milii magnitudine, rotun-dus, niger, splendens. Totum autem corpus, crura & alae sunt insignis splendentis coloris, ex nigro, viridi, & aureo mixti; estque totum subtilissimis pilis vestitum.

Validissimus est, nam scatulae crassae à me inclusus, ac latere cocto crasso imposito nihilo-minus se semper exserebat, ut funiculis fuerit coërcendus. Hirci pene odorem de se fundit.

TAVRVS volans alius. Crura habet sex, quatuor in posteriore, & duo in anteriore se-ctione corporis: pedes desinunt in duo lunata cornicula: singulaque habent tenuius tenacu-lum. Anterior sectio digitum longa in cornu desinit duos & semis digitos longum, teres & paulum deorsum incurvatum, & duos habens veluti dentes versus posteriora. Inferius in an-tica parte corporis, sub exortu hujus cornu, jungitur caput, parvum quidem, sed & cornu habens sursum incurvatum, duos fere digitos longum, cum processu tripartito in ipso acu-mine. Oculos habet rotundos, nigros, splendentes, seminis cannabini magnitudine, pone oculos autem duos processus coniformes, contortos, posterior sectio duos digitos est longa, atque alis crassis tecta, cum anterior sectio glabra & solida testa tegatur quae & in cornu exten-ditur.

66 ▪ HERCULES BEETLE *Dynastes sp.*

"Taurus volans alius." Woodcut. In *Historia naturalis Brasiliae . . .* by Willem Piso and Georges Marcgrave (1658). ▪ The Dynastid beetles include some of the largest insects, such as the aptly named Hercules and rhinoceros beetles, which are generally distinguished by the large "horns" of the males. All are scarab beetles, members of the enormous family that also includes the sacred scarab of ancient Egypt and the highly destructive Japanese Beetle. Piso and Marcgrave's early work on the natural history and medicine of Brazil was for one hundred and fifty years the only source of information on Brazilian zoology. It was based on explorations in 1637 of the northeastern regions of what was then a Dutch colony.

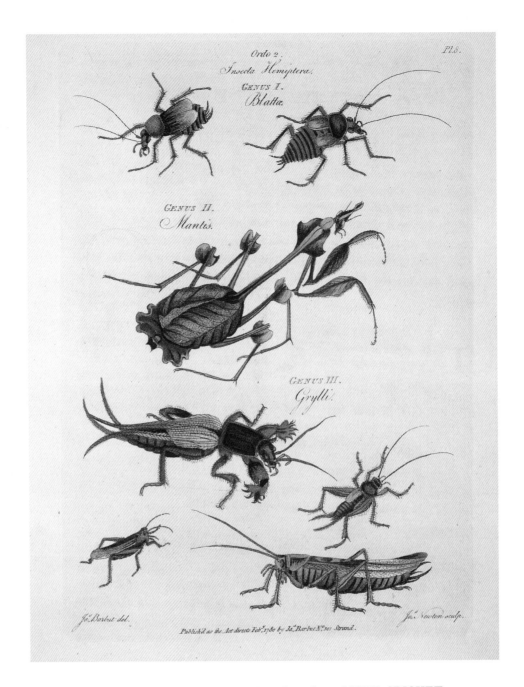

67 • MANTIS Order *Mantodea* ▪ COCKROACH Order *Blattodea* ▪ MOLE-CRICKET ▪
GRASSHOPPER Order *Orthoptera*

Hand-colored engraving, by James Newton from drawing by James Barbut. In *Les genres des Insectes de Linné . . .* by
James Barbut (1781). ▪ *Genres* is a free translation into both English and French from part of the thirteenth edition
of Carolus Linnaeus's bible of modern taxonomy, *Systema naturae*. It is illustrated with Barbut's beautifully drawn if
not always accurate renderings of British insects. Featured in a group that includes a cockroach and a mole-cricket is a
mantis which looks like a leaf. Although now called either Preying (for its predatory behavior) or Praying (for its
appearance) Mantis, Barbut called it the "Soothsayer" because "this insect by stretching out its fore feet, divined and
pointed out those things that were asked of it."

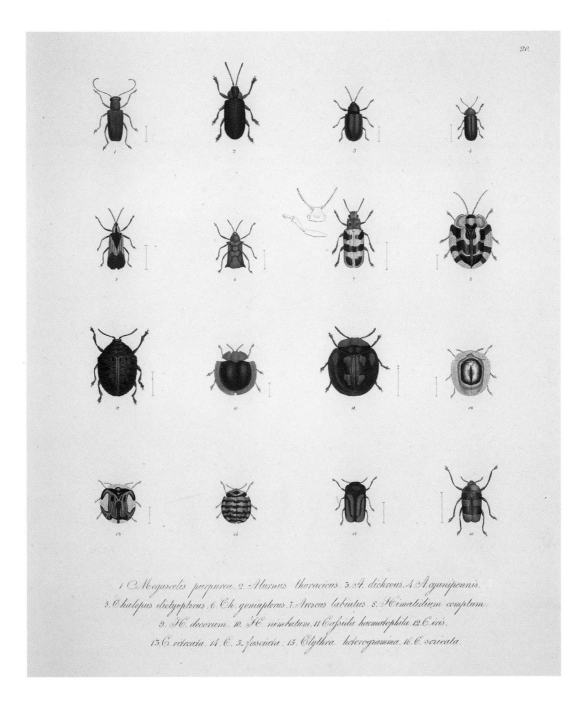

1 Megascelis purpurea. 2 Alurnus thoracicus. 3 A. dichrous. 4 A. cyanipennis.
5 Chalepus dictyopterus. 6 Ch. goniapterus. 7 Arescus labiatus. 8 Himatidium comptum.
9 H. decorum. 10 H. nimbatum. 11 Cassida haematophila. 12 C. iris.
13 C. vitreata. 14 C. 5-fasciata. 15 Clythra heterogramma. 16 C. sericata.

68 · LEAF BEETLES Family *Chrysomelidae*

Hand-colored etching, by Wilhelm Siegrist from uncredited drawing. In *Delectus animalium articulatorum . . .* by Johann Baptist von Spix (1830–34). ▪ Of the at least one and a quarter million *known* species of living animals, some 70–80 percent are insects. Of these, approximately 300,000 species are beetles. The most obvious distinguishing feature of the order Coleoptera are the elytra, the horny wing covers that meet in a straight line down the back and hide the membranous flying wings. These sixteen jewel-like insects all belong to the fourth largest Coleoptera family, the Chrysomelidae or leaf beetles, a group that also includes such well-known agricultural pests as potato, asparagus, and cucumber beetles.

69 ▪ POLYPHEMUS MOTH *Antheraea polyphemus*, and other moths

"A.B. Polyphemus; C.D. Syringa; E.F. Progne." Hand-colored engraving, from drawing by Pieter Cramer. In *Sammlung und Beschreibung ausländischer Schmetterlinge . . .* by Pieter Cramer (1788). ▪ *Papillons exotiques*, as Cramer's *Sammlung* is also known, has parallel German and French texts; other editions of his popular study were issued in Dutch and French. Cramer arranged his subjects in pretty, geometrical patterns, with dorsal and ventral views of each insect. Featured in this illustration is the large, showy Polyphemus Moth, whose wingspan averages five inches. Cramer noted that it was found in New York and in Jamaica.

70 · LANTERN FLY OR PEANUTHEAD *Lanternaria phosphorea*

"Porte-Lanterne." Hand-colored engraving, by J. Mülder from drawing by Maria Sibylla Merian. In *Dissertation sur la génération et les transformations des insectes de Surinam . . .* by Maria Sibylla Merian (1726). · Maria Merian abandoned her husband to join a religious sect and then, inspired by the beauty of butterflies, traveled to the Dutch colony of Surinam to paint the native insects and flora. Her highly decorative renderings are the first records of the spectacular transformations of many insects, shown among their food plants. The lantern flies, named for their large head protuberances, were once erroneously thought to be luminescent, like fireflies. They are actually fulgorids, or planthoppers.

PL.XXVIII

71 ▪ BUTTERFLIES AND MOTHS

Hand-colored engraving, by Moses Harris from his own drawing. In *The Aurelian . . .* by Moses Harris (1840). ▪
The euphonious title of *The Aurelian* derives from the Latin "aureolus," meaning golden, and refers to the iridescent
color of many chrysalids. Fluttering about the Scabiosa plant are moths (k. Lesser Treble Bar, l. Crimson and Gold,
m. Speckled Yellow) and butterflies (c-d. High Brown Fritillary, e-i. Marsh Fritillary). Harris called the last
"Dishclout, or Greasey Fritillaria" because "the under Side of the upper Wing always appears greasey."

II.
LYCÆNIDÆ.

W. C. Hewitson, del. et lith. 1860   Printed by Hullmandel & Walton

1. 2. 3. AMBLYPODIA AMANTES   7. 8. 9. AMBLYPODIA AMYTIS
4. 5. 6. AMBLYPODIA MENANDER   10. 11. 12. 13. AMBLYPODIA CENTAURUS.

72 ▪ GOSSAMER WINGED BUTTERFLIES *1–3. Amblypodia amantes, 4–6. A. menander,*
7–9. A. amytis, 10–13. A. centaurius

"Lycaenidae." Hand-colored lithograph, by William C. Hewitson. In *Specimens of a catalogue of Lycaenidae in the British Museum* by William C. Hewitson (1862). ▪ For simplicity, these Lycenid butterflies, probably tropical members of a large group with worldwide distribution, are referred to as Blues. The larvae of some Blues are predators, unlike most caterpillars, which feed on plants. In contrast to this study, Hewitson also prepared exhaustive catalogues documenting the extensive lepidoptera collections of the British Museum.

SATYRUS.
III.

ALOPE.
Form NEPHELE, 1.2 ♂, 3.4 ♀.
Var: OLYMPUS, 5 ♂, 6 ♀; a. Larva (mature) b. Chrysalis.
7-13 intergrades.

73 ▪ WOOD NYMPH *Cercyonis alope*

"Satyrus Alope." Hand-colored lithograph, from drawing by Mary Peart. In *The butterflies of North America* by William Henry Edwards (1868–97). ▪ The members of the butterfly family *Satyridae*, called Satyrs or Wood Nymphs, are medium-sized, brown, and usually have "eyespots" on both sets of wings. Like their mythical namesakes they inhabit woodlands, and because of their fast, irregular flight patterns they are very difficult to catch.

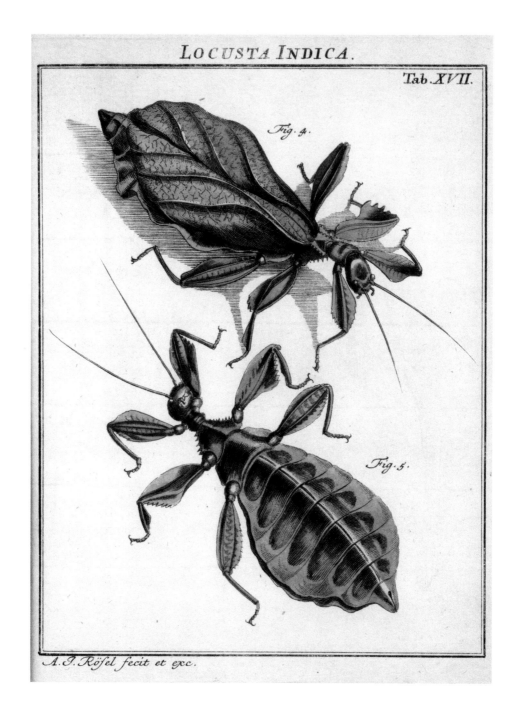

74 ▪ LEAF INSECTS *Phyllium sp.*

"Locusta Indica." Hand-colored engraving, by Augustin Roesel von Rosenhof from his own drawing. In *Der Monatlich Herausgegeben Insectenbelustigung . . .* by Augustin Roesel von Rosenhof (1746–61). ▪ Merian's "Insects of Surinam" inspired Roesel, a painter of miniatures, to devote his life to studying and painting insects, although he took time out to produce a classic illustrated study of frogs and toads. *Insecten,* unfinished upon his death in 1759, was completed by his collaborator and son-in-law, Christian Frederick Kleeman, who together with Roesel's daughter, Katharina Barbara, colored the more than 2,200 figures in the four volumes and supplements. Leaf insects are examples of a very effective means of animal camouflage by mimicking the surrounding vegetation.

1 et 1 b *Heliconius Duvalii* 2 et 2 b *Acraca Phlegetontia*.
3 et 3 b *Polyommatus valens* 4 et 4 b *Biblis Hesperia*.
5 et 5 b *Hesperia versicolor* 6 et 6 b *H. St. Hilarii*.
7. *Castnia Latreillei*

75 ▪ BUTTERFLIES, SKIPPERS, MOTH

Hand-colored etching, by Wilhelm Siegrist from uncredited drawing. In *Delectus animalium articulatorum . . .* by Johann Baptist von Spix (1830–34). ▪ Zoologist Johann von Spix and botanist Phillip van Martius amassed large collections of animal and plant specimens during their explorations in Brazil from 1817 to 1820. These were described and illustrated in Spix's subsequent publications on birds, monkeys, and, in *Delectus*, on Brazilian insects. Some of the problems of lepidoptera classification are exemplified in this grouping. The diurnal skippers, with moth-like bodies, are named for their erratic flight patterns and are often grouped with butterflies. The luminously colored central figure, *Castnia latreille*, is a moth that resembles a skipper, and has been described as having more butterfly-like characteristics than some butterflies.

76 • BUGS Order *Homoptera*

"Insectes Hémiptères." Hand-colored etching, by Fournier from drawing by Blanchard. In *Dictionnaire universel d'histoire naturelle* edited by Alcide Dessalines d'Orbigny (1839–49). ▪ Although insects are sometimes referred to as "bugs," especially by people who don't like them, true bugs are members of specific orders, such as the Homoptera, distinguished by jointed beaks emerging from their heads that are used for sucking juices, usually from plants. Cicadas, treehoppers, spittlebugs, aphids, whiteflies, and leafhoppers, such as the big-headed lantern fly depicted here, are all members of this enormous order. Paris's Muséum National d'Histoire Naturelle sponsored the extraordinary explorations through all of South America led by d'Orbigny from 1826 to 1833.

OUTCASTS, COLD-BLOODED AND BEAUTIFUL

The cold-blooded animals are, in a basic way, the undeserving victims of mankind's ingratitude. If they are not feared and hated by men, as snakes are, they are mocked and scorned as frogs and toads are. Yet if it weren't for some ancient, cold-blooded kin, man himself might not be here. Back in the dimmest of pasts, after fish had learned to live on land and amphibians had developed, the first reptiles evolved. Some went on to become the huge dinosaurs that once dominated the earth and, through them, evolved into birds. Others became the snakes, crocodiles, and lizards known today. And one historic but still unidentified reptile evolved into a mammal, and, eventually, into man. Ungratefulness, as Shakespeare aptly observed, is "sharper than a serpent's tooth." ▪ The Bible set the first curse on snakes—"upon your belly you shall go," said the Lord to the serpent of Eden, "and dust you shall eat all the days of your life." But not all cultures turned their backs on reptiles. In Buddhist belief it was the serpent that, coiling itself under a meditating Buddha, held him safely up out of the great flood. To Hindus, snakes were symbols of fertility and wisdom. In Egypt, crocodiles were worshipped as protectors of the Nile. ▪ Psychologists today, trying to come to disinterested conclusions, are not sure if the fear of snakes is a genetic or a cultural phenomenon. Relatively few snakes are venomous and fewer still can crush their prey. They are regarded as slippery and slimy but their skins actually have a dry satiny feel as pleasant to stroke as any cat's fur. ▪ Gifted artists have found a strange beauty in reptiles—in the colorful snakes, the awesome alligators, the gawky frogs. Edward Lear's turtles have a real-life attractiveness. Mark Catesby painted enchanting frogs and snakes of the American south. ▪ Nobody is really afraid of the snake's cold-blooded companions in nature, the frogs and toads known, in zoology, as batrachians. But nobody gives them much respect either. The fairy tale frog, as the ultimate in ugliness, needs an uncommon act of compassion to be turned back into a handsome prince. The English in particular for a long while had no use for frogs. One eminent naturalist warned against "the wanton eating of frogs" as "perilous to life and health" while other Englishmen went out of their way to insult Hollanders by referring to frogs as "Dutch nightingales." ▪ That fearsome reptile of legend is represented here by a namesake, *Draco volans*, the Flying Dragon, which earns its name with its appearance. Its innocent habits and temperament might shame its mythical ancestors. Where the original dragon went around abducting maidens and snorting flames at rescuers, *Draco volans* glides timidly from tree to tree, trying to keep out of the way of predatory birds, which are its mortal enemies, and hunting for ants, which are its favorite food.

77 · MEDITERRANEAN CHAMELEON *Chamaeleo chamaeleon* [?]

"De Chamaeleonte." Woodcut. In *Historiae animalium* by Conrad Gesner (1551–87). ▪ Chameleons are small lizards, known for their ability to change color to blend with their background, a device that camouflages them from both their predators and the insects that they snatch with their coiled, sticky tongue. Binocular vision also sets them apart from other lizards: each protruding eye can swivel in its socket independently of the other.

Pl. XXXIII. pag. 447.

DeSève del.

venue Tardieu sc.

LE DRAGON *grandeur de Nature.*

78 ▪ **FLYING DRAGON** *Draco volans*

"Le Dragon." Etching, by Tardieu from drawing by J. E. DeSève. In *Histoire naturelle . . .* by Le Comte de Buffon (1746–1804). ▪ The patagium, folds of skin supported umbrella-fashion by elongated ribs, enable this unusual lizard to glide from tree to tree. When not in use the structure folds neatly away from sight. DeSève attempted to impart life to this Draco specimen by setting it in a tree, not unlike those of the hot, humid rain forests native to the lizard.

PTYCHEMYS RUGOSA Ag.

79 ▪ REDBELLY TURTLE *Pseudemys rubriventris*

"Ptychemys Rugosa." Hand-colored lithograph, by A. Sonrel from drawing by Jacques Burkhardt. In *Contributions to the natural history of the United States of America* by Louis Agassiz (1857–62). ▪ Swiss-born Louis Agassiz's American career centered around Harvard University where he founded its Museum of Comparative Zoology, wrote the popular *Principles of Zoology* (1848), and began *Contributions*, of which only four of ten projected volumes were completed. Volume 2 is devoted entirely to North American turtles. These Redbelly Turtles frequent ponds, lakes, and streams of the eastern United States, feeding on aquatic vegetation and small water creatures.

Lacerta.

Tab: LXXVI

Eÿdexen.

Lacerta Chalcidica flexuosa

Lacerta.

Lacerta Biceps

Lacertus Biceps

Lacert₉ Viridis Liguro Bononiensibus

Lacert₉ Viridis Caudâ bifurcâ.

Lacertus Viridis exiccatus Caudâ bifida.

Lacertæ et Stelliones

Lacertæ et Stelliones.

Lacertus Cÿprius Scincoides.

80 ▪ FANCIFUL LIZARDS

Engraving, by Matthaeus Merian from his own drawing. In *Historia naturalis de quadrupedibus . . .* by John Jonston (1653). ▪ Superb illustrations by Matthaeus Merian, father of Maria Sibylla Merian, were an important reason for the enormous popularity of Jonston's fanciful plagiarizations of the works of Gesner and Aldrovandi. Among these twelve lizards is one especially imaginative creature, adorned with a trail of stars down his back. The unlikely looking forked tails of three of the animals do occur in nature, largely as the result of regeneration following an injury.

81 ▪ HATCHLING CROCODILES *Crocodylus sp*

Engraving. In *Locupletissimi rerum naturalium thesauri . . .* by Albert Seba (1734–65). ▪ Reptiles figured prominently in Seba's extensive collection of natural history objects, and are the predominant images in volumes 1 and 2 of his massive catalogue. What appears to be a scene of a crocodile nursery is actually a developmental sequence study of one species, probably the American Crocodile *Crocodylus acutus* (nos. 1–9), together with the young of either the Estuarine Crocodile *C. porosum*, or the Mugger Crocodile *C. palustris* (nos. 10,11). The remaining figure is very likely a member of one of these three species.

T. 72.

Rana maxima   *Helleborona*

82 ▪ BULLFROG *Rana catesbiana*

"The Bull Frog." Hand-colored etching, by Mark Catesby from his own drawing. In *The Natural History of Carolina, Florida and the Bahama Islands* . . . by Mark Catesby (2d ed., 1754). ▪ The most famous illustrated book of American plant and animal life earned for its author/artist/engraver the title "Father of American Ornithology." Although half of the 220 plates depict birds set among native American plants, the balance portray with equal charm and beauty of design the reptiles, fishes, insects, mammals, and amphibians of the southern colonies, including this vigorous Bullfrog, depicted with a Yellow Lady Slipper. In 1802 the English naturalist George Shaw named the Bullfrog *Rana catesbiana* in honor of Catesby.

1 *Hyla Viridis.* 2 *Rana Esculenta.* 3 *Rana Temporaria.*

Petrus Quattrocchi del. 1837.

Romae Lith. Battistelli

83 ▪ COMMON TREE FROG *Hyla arborea* ▪ EDIBLE FROG *Rana esculenta* ▪
COMMON FROG *R. temporaria*

"1. Hyla Viridis; 2. Rana Esculenta; 3. Rana Temporaria." Hand-colored lithograph, by Battistelli from drawing by Petrus Quattrocchi. In *Iconografia della fauna italica . . .* by Charles-Lucien Bonaparte (1832–41). ▪ Napoleon's nephew was a distinguished naturalist who authored several important illustrated books on various subjects: a continuation of Alexander Wilson's *American Ornithology* (1825–33), a monograph on pigeons (1857–58), and this monumental three-volume survey of the vertebrates of Italy, illustrated with 180 lithographs of mammals, birds, fish, reptiles, and amphibians.

Pl. IX. pag. 267.

De Seve d.   Chevillet !

LA GÉOMÉTRIQUE, grandeur de moitié de Nature.

84 ▪ GEOMETRIC TORTOISE *Psammobates geometricus*

"La Géométrique." Etching, by Chevillet from drawing by J. E. DeSève. In *Histoire naturelle . . .* by Le Comte de Buffon (1746–1804). ▪ The artist, DeSève, who also illustrated many editions of Buffon's masterwork, provided full backgrounds, including classical landscapes complete with architectural ruins, for the hundreds of animals he depicted in the forty-four volumes of the first edition of *Histoire naturelle*. The aptly named Geometric Tortoise is found in South Africa. Like most tortoises, it is primarily herbivorous.

EMYS SCABRA.

J.D.C.Sowerby del.E.Lear lithog.   Printed by C.Hullmandel

85 ▪ GUIANA WOOD TURTLE *Rhinoclemmys punctularia punctularia*

"Emys Scabra." Lithograph, by Edward Lear from drawing by James de Carle Sowerby. In *Tortoises, terrapins and turtles drawn from life . . .* by John Edward Gray (1872). ▪ This semiterrestrial turtle of the South American rain forests is one of 60 illustrations that Edward Lear lithographed from Sowerby's drawings for *Tortoises*. Gray, director of the British Museum's natural history section and editor of many of its catalogues, had worked with Lear before, when he wrote *Gleanings from the Menagerie and Aviary at Knowsley Hall* (1846), a collection of Lear's animal art created while he lived on the estate of the Earl of Derby.

86 ▪ CAIMAN OR CROCODILE

"Crocodile de Suriname." Hand-colored etching. In *Dissertation sur la génération et les transformations des insectes de Surinam . . .* by Maria Sibylla Merian (1726). ▪ This fanciful illustration of a lizard-clawed and tailed crocodilian entwined with a snake comes as a surprise in a book famed for its glorious depictions of flowers and insects. The plate did not appear in the 1705 first edition, nor is it the work of Maria Merian or her daughters. It derives, instead, from similar work in Albert Seba's *Locupletissimi. . . .* The caiman, a close relative of the alligator, "is feared by the natives—it eats everything it encounters," wrote Merian.

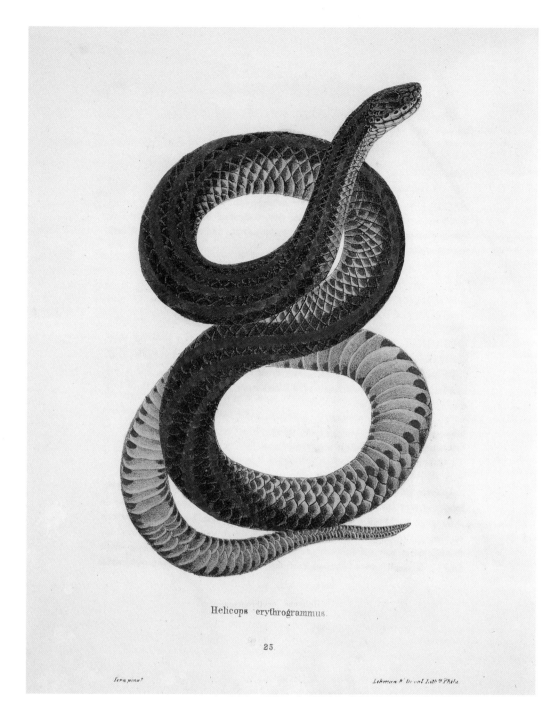

Helicops erythrogrammus.

25

Sera pinx.   Libman & Duval Lith. & Phila.

87 ▪ RAINBOW SNAKE *Farancia erytrogramma*

"Helicops erythrogrammus." Hand-colored lithograph, by Libman & Duval from drawing by Sera. In *North American herpetology . . .* by John Edward Holbrook (1842). ▪ The multi-colored Rainbow Snake, which ranges in size from three to six feet, is found in swampy areas, and in and around rivers and streams where eels are its principal food. It is the "hoop snake" of American tall tales that rolls itself into a circle by biting its own tail. Holbrook's exhaustive, five-volume study of the reptiles and amphibians of the eastern United States remains a classic resource in its field.

NAJA TRIPUDIANS.

Bunshunnah Kaultiah.
from left
Length 4.3 circum 4"

Plate 3

Drawn by Annoda Prosad Bagchee Student

HANHART CHLMO LITH

Gov Sch of Art Calcutta

88 ▪ SPECTACLED COBRA *Naja naja*

"Naja Tripudians." Chromolithograph, by Hanhart from drawing by Annoda Prosad Bagchee. In *The thanatophidia of India* by Joseph Fayrer (1874). ▪ *Thanatophidia* not only describes the poisonous snakes of India but was the authoritative treatise of this period on snakebite and its treatments. Fayrer, a physician noted for his extensive writings on tropical and Indian diseases and health care, claimed that venomous snakes took the lives of some 20,000 Indians annually. All the illustrations for *Thanatophidia* were drawn from life by native students of the Government School of Art in Calcutta.

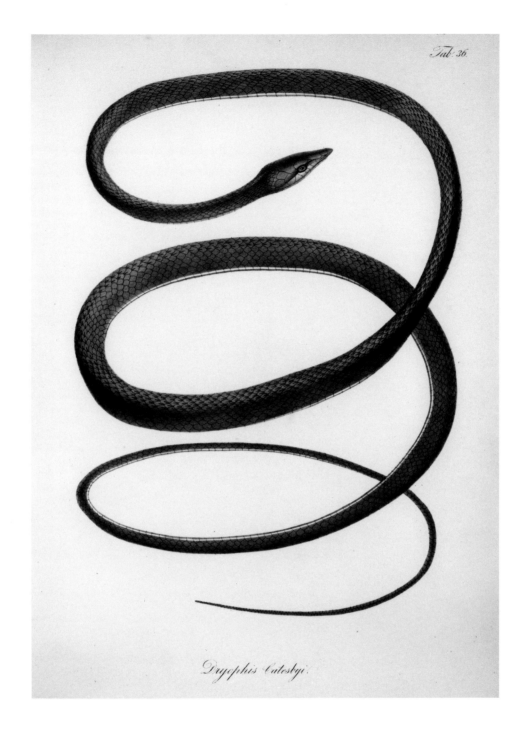

Tab. 36.

Dryophis Catesbyi.

89 ▪ VINE SNAKE *Oxybelis fulgidus*

"Dryophis Catesbyi." Hand-colored lithograph. In *Abbildungen neuer oder unvollständig* by Hermann Schlegel (1837–44). ▪ Mark Catesby's influence and importance is again evident here: this mildly venomous tree snake was originally named after Catesby. The snake, found in the warm forests of Central and South America, is approximately five feet long, and is almost indistinguishable from the surrounding flora. Schlegel, who also served as director of the natural history museum in Leiden, published classic works in subjects other than herpetology, including a general natural history and a study of the birds of the Netherlands as well as of those of the Dutch Indies.

Early in the twelfth century, St. Bernard of Clairvaux, the most powerful churchman of his time, turned his wrath on a host of creatures that had invaded his monastery, their likenesses carved in its walls and pillars. "Monstrous centaurs," he thundered, "animals with many bodies under one head or many heads on a single body . . . a four-footed beast with a serpent's tail . . . fish with a beast's head. We are more tempted to read in marble than in our books!" Going on practical considerations he concluded: "For God's sake, if men are not ashamed of their follies, why at least do they not shrink from the expense." ▪ Bernard's exasperation was wasted because these follies had for centuries been embedded in men's beliefs as the subjects of the most gripping stories and compelling art. A world of strange animals had been bred out of a millennium of confused observation and uninhibited imagining—manticores with a man's head and a scorpion's tail, the ravenous harpy with a virgin's face, and a hydra with seven heads. ▪ The great perpetrator of these misbegotten myths was a writer who went by the name of Physiologus. Around the fourth century he put together a natural history based on both sober scientific and historical works and the chronicles of credulous travelers. Eminent scholars accepted Physiologus and it became the source of popular medieval books called bestiaries. ▪ Often the imaginary animal was engendered by earnest but faulty descriptions. The ypo-

CURIOUS CREATURES, REAL AND IMAGINED

tain, or hippopotamus, was transformed from its placid herbivorous self into an animal with hoofs like an ox, a mane like a horse, a neigh like a wild ass's, and a terrifying appetite for human beings. The unicorn had a long horn in its forehead that could impale any opponent and a bray that turned a brave man's courage into panic. ▪ Few men, if any, had ever seen a unicorn but then very few men in Europe had ever seen a rhinoceros so that it was as easy to accept one as the other. Albrecht Dürer, the most impeccable of artists, had not seen one when he did his portrait of a rhinoceros, embodying all the misconceptions about the animal and endowing it with overlapping plates of armored hide and an extra tusk. ▪ Just as the Renaissance was debunking the myths explorers started coming back from the new worlds with descriptions of animals that could no more be believed than those in Physiologus. People who had been told to forget the manticore were now confronted with something called an armadillo—"a beast armed," the report said, "and, in the snoute, like unto a pig . . . a great tayle like to a lizard. . . ." ▪ And hoax was written all over a creature discovered in Australia around 1780. It had the body of a mole, the webbed feet of a water fowl, the bill of a duck. It laid and hatched eggs but nursed its young. This implausible animal had a hard time establishing its credentials. After all, with the harpy discredited and the hydra banished to the land of legend, no one in his right mind would fall for something called the duck billed platypus.

maſſe, ſalua eſſe omnia ſi Satyrus & Cupido ſupereſſent, ita côfeſſione iudicij dolo expreſſa, fœminæ Cupidinem optanti non Satyrum dediſſe,&c. Hæc ille ex Atticis Pauſaniæ. Protogenes Rhodius pinxit Satyrū quem Anapauómenon uocant, tibias tenentem, Plinius. Celebratur & Stratonicus, qui Satyrum in phiala grauatum ſomno collocauiſſe uerius, ĉḡ cælaſſe dictus eſt, Idem. Timanthes pinxit Cyclopem dormiente in paruula tabella, atcḡ iuxta Satyros thyrſo pollicê eius metientes, Idê.

¶ Satyri cuiuſdam adulatoris utriuſcḡ Dionyſij meminit Timæus, Athenæus. Satyri architecti mentio apud Plinium 36. 9. Satyrus Eleus, Lyſianactis fil. ex genere lamidarum, quinquies in Nemea pugiles uicit, in Pythijs bis, bis inſuper in Olympia. ſtatuā eius fecit Silanion Athenienſis, Pauſanias in Eliacis. Gorgippus filius Satyri tyranni Boſpori, Polyænus lib. 8. Strateg. Satyrus quidam medicus Galeni præceptor fuit. ¶ Satyra nomen ſcorti Attici, Σατύρα, Athenæo lib. 13. ¶ Herodianus ſcribit Helotas quocḡ appellari ſatyros, qui ſint apud Tænarum. Erāt uero Helotæ publici quodammodo Lacedæmoniorum ſerui,&c. Cælius. Satyrorum inſulæ, Σατύρων νῆσοι, ſunt tres contra Indiam, extra Gangen ſitæ, Ptolemæo 2. 7. quas qui habitant caudas habere dicuntur, quales Satyris pinguntur, Pauſanias has inſulas Satyrias uocat, (Cælius Satyrides transfert,) cuius uerba ſuperius hac ipſa in parte retuli. Satyrion, regio prope Tarentum, gentile Satyrinus, Stephanus. Satura ſeu Satyra palus Pontina eſt, uigintiquatuor urbium olim locus capax. Qua Saturæ iacet atra palus, gelidusĉḡ per imas   Quærit iter ualles, atcḡ in mare conditur Vfens, Vergil. 7. Aen. Cælius. Meminit huius paludis etiam Plinius 3. 6. Satyrus fluuius in Aquitania, cuius meminit Lucanus lib. 1. Tunc rura Nemetis   Qui tenet,& ripas Satyri qua littore curua.

¶ Finitimos Indiæ montes tranſmittenti, ad intimum latus denſiſſimas conualles uideri aiunt, & Corudam locum nominari, ubi beſtiæ ſatyrorum ſimilitudinem formamĉḡ gerentes, & toto corpore hirſutæ, uerſantur: atque equina cauda præditæ dicuntur. Eæ cum non à uenatoribus agitantur, in opacis & ſpiſſis ſyluis ſolent uiuere. Cum autem uenantium ſtrepitum ſentiunt, & canum latratus exaudiunt, in montium uertices incredibili celeritate recurrunt: nam per montes iter conficere aſſuetæ ſunt. Contra eos qui ſe inſequuntur pugnant, de ſummis montibus ſaxa deuoluentes. Ex ijs nonnullæ, ſed ægerrime tandem, aut ægrotantes, aut grauidæ comprehenduntur. Illæ quidem propter morbum: hæ uero ob grauiditatem, Aelianus. Sed feras toto corpore hirtas eſſe, caudis equinis, & propter celeritatem non niſi morbo aut ſenecta graues capi, alij authores ſatyris ipſis attribuerūt.

Monſtri huius deſcriptio proxima pagina ſequitur.

¶ In Syluis Saxoniæ uerſus Daciam, in deſerto murice (nemore) cuiuſdā, capta ſunt parum ante hæc tempora duo monſtra piloſa, ferê in omnibus habentia figuram hominis: & fœmina quidê mortua fuit morſibus canum & uulneribus uenatorum. Maſculus autem captus eſt domeſticus, & didicit ire ſuper pedes erectus: & didicit loqui imperfectê ualde & non multa uerba, & habuit uocê exilem ſicut capreolus, & rationem nullam habuit, de ſeceſſu & egeſtione & alijs talibus uerecundabatur, multum autem appetijt coire cum mulieribus, & has publice qualeſcuncḡ eſſent tempore libidinis opprimere tentauit, Albertus. Et rurſus libro 22. in Catalogo quadrupedum, de Confuſa beſtia ſcribens, citatis Solini uerbis; quæ apud Solinum non de Confuſa (corruptum enim hoc nomen eſt)

90 · SATYR

Woodcut. In *Historiae animalium* by Conrad Gesner (1551–87). ▪ Although Gesner began the study of zoology as a modern science with his encyclopedic *Historiae animalium*, he covered a fair amount of superstitious baggage from the past—mythological monsters, such as this satyr, and fabulous beasts were included. The classical man/beast was a shy woodland spirit, companion to the demigod Pan, who delighted in dancing and consorting with nymphs and any available human women.

28 Monstrum Marinum effigie Monachi.

91 · MONK FISH

"Monstrum Marinum effigie Monachi." Woodcut. In *Opera omnia* by Ulisse Aldrovandi (1599–1668). ▪ Not only fabulous beasts and fantastic creatures, but also freaks of nature populate the "monster" volume of Aldrovandi's natural world encyclopedia. Vivid woodcuts of Siamese twins, three-legged chickens, and other oddities embellish its pages. This "finned" monastic perpetuates the medieval notion that everything on earth and in the air has its counterpart in the waters. There is even a Bishop Fish.

Monſtrorum Hiſtoria. 337

Alioquin iuxta veritatem hiſtoricam, Chymæra mons Lyciæ igniuomus fuiſſe
perhibetur, in cuius faſtigio leones verſabantur, mediam montis partem paſcuam
capræ colebant, & demum circa radices montis ſerpentes nidulabantur. Hinc fa-
ctus eſt fabulæ locus, chymęram fuiſſe monſtrum, cuius pars antica erat leonina,
media caprina, & poſtica ſerpentina;& quoniam Bellerophontes Glauci filius ſum-
ma diligentia hunc montem habitabilem reddidit: propterea Priſci hoc immane,&
efferum monſtrum à Bel lerophonte mactatum fuiſſe monimentis mandarunt.

Præterea extat quædam Bembi tabula, cuius titulus eſt. Typus vetuſtiſſimæ ta-
E   bulæ eneæ hieroglyphicis, nimirum ſacris Aegyptiorum litteris exaratæ, in qua,
ad publicam vtilitatem, monſtrificæ animantes expreſſę conſpiciuntur, quæ non
modò monſtroſæ, ſed etiam, vt noſtra fert opinio, fabuloſæ eſſe videntur: cum
ibi multa cernantur animalium ſimulacra, quæ partim ex lineamentis auium, partim
ex lineamentis quadrupedum integrantur. Libuit autem iſthæc hoc in loco ſpe-
ctanda proponere, vt nihil noſtræ monſtrorum hiſtoriæ deeſſet. Primitùs hæc tabula quatuor Harpyarum ſpecies referre videtur. Quandoquidem ἅρπυαι rapaces
quædam Deæ ab Antiquis eſſe credebantur, deducto nomine à verbo ἁρπάζω ra-
pio. Sed Heſiodus in Theogonia ſcriptum reliquit Harpyas fuiſſe Dæmonia ala-

Tabula Bē-
bi.

Harpyæqua
fuerint.

Harpyæ prima icon.

F f   ta,

92 · HARPY

"Harpyae prima icon." Woodcut. In *Opera omnia* by Ulisse Aldrovandi (1559–1668). ▪ Virgil described the
Harpies of Greek mythology as loathsome, taloned birds with hags' faces and breasts, and bears' ears, who snatched
mortals away to the Underworld—a far cry from the beautiful winged goddesses from even earlier times, who were
swifter than the winds. Aldrovandi's Harpy, copied from a pre-existing image, is an odd creature, though much
pleasanter in appearance than Virgil's foul, fearsome monster.

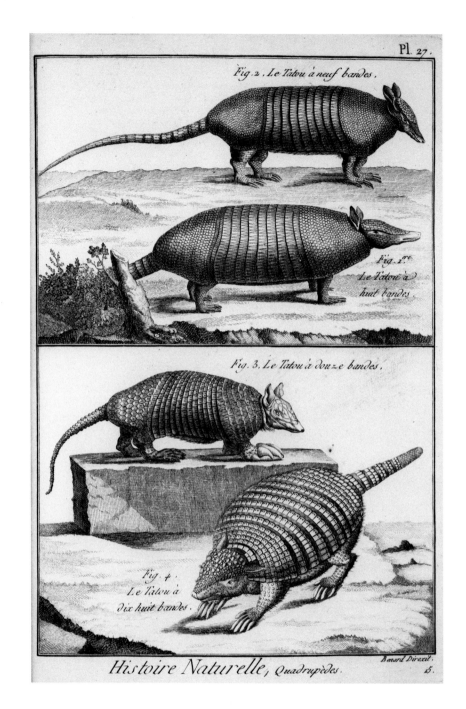

Pl. 27.

Fig. 2. Le Tatou à neuf bandes.

Fig. 1re. Le Tatou à huit bandes.

Fig. 3. Le Tatou à douze bandes.

Fig. 4. Le Tatou à dix huit bandes.

Histoire Naturelle, Quadrupèdes.

Benard Direxit.
15.

93 ▪ NINE-BANDED ARMADILLO *Dasypus novemcinctus* ▪
NAKED TAILED ARMADILLO *Cabassous unicinctus?* ▪ HAIRY ARMADILLO *Chaetophractus villosus*

"Le Tatou à huit . . . , neuf . . . , douze . . . , dix huit bandes." Etching, by Benard from drawing by J. E. DeSève. In *Encyclopédie methodique . . .* (1774–1832), vol. 135: *Mammalogie* by Anselme-Gaetan Desmarest (1820). ▪ Armadillo is the Spanish diminutive of "armored" and accurately describes the bony plates covered with thick skin that protect these odd mammals from most predators. Rolling into a tight ball is the well-known defense strategy of some species: others flatten themselves against the ground, pulling their legs out of harm's way. Large, powerful claws enable armadillos to burrow swiftly away from danger.

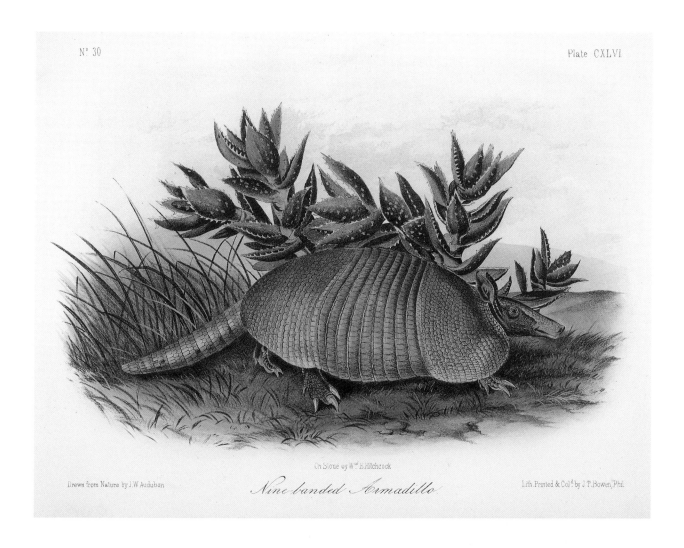

On Stone by Wm. E. Hitchcock

Drawn from Nature by J.W Audubon   *Nine-banded Armadillo*   Lith. Printed & Colᵈ by J.T. Bowen, Phil

94 ▪ NINE-BANDED ARMADILLO *Dasypus novemcinctus*

"Nine-banded Armadillo." Hand-colored lithograph, by William E. Hitchcock from drawing by John Woodhouse Audubon. In *The quadrupeds of North America* by John James Audubon and John Bachman (1849–54). ▪ The creation of *Quadrupeds* was very much a family affair. Reverend Bachman was father-in-law to Audubon's sons, John Woodhouse and Victor. The former painted many of the animal portraits, while Victor published both the first, large edition (1845–48) and this octavo set. According to coauthors John James Audubon and John Bachman, this armored mammal "resembles a small pig saddled with the shell of a turtle."

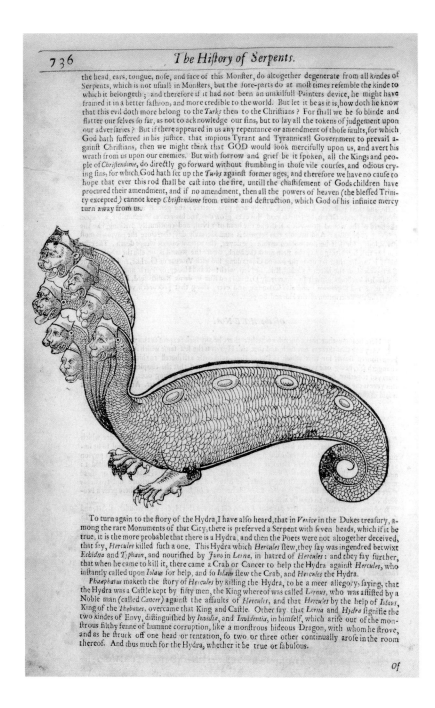

95 · HYDRA

Engraving. In *The History of four-footed beasts and serpents . . .* by Edward Topsell (1658). ▪ This image of the Hydra, a fearsome many-headed monster from Greek mythology, appeared first in Gesner's *Historiae animalium* and then in Topsell's translation and adaptation, with both authors acknowledging that it was an imaginary creature. In the eighteenth century a similar image appeared, in Albert Seba's *Locupletissimi*, as documentation of the notorious "Hamburg Hydra." That Hydra had been a local tourist attraction until Carolus Linnaeus came to Nuremberg and exposed it as a hoax, having been created from sewn-together parts of different animals. Seba purchased the discredited "monster" as an appropriate addition to his vast "cabinet of curiosities."

Tab. XII

Draco ex Raia effictus
Aldrou.

Draco alter ex Raia   exsiccata concinnatus.
Aldro.

Basiliscus in solitudine Africæ viuens
Aldro.

Basiliscus ex Raia effictus proné   et supiné pictus
Aldro.

96 • DRAGONS AND BASILISKS

"1. Draco ex Raia . . . ; 2. Draco alter ex Raia . . . ; 3. Basiliscus in solitudine . . . ; 4. Basiliscus ex Raia. . . ."
Engraving, by Matthaeus Merian from his own drawing. In *Historia naturalis . . . de serpentibus . . .* by John Jonston
(1653). ▪ Jonston, unlike his more usual casual approach to documentation, acknowledged in his captions that these
dragons and basilisks derived from rays, winged fish with long stinging tails. Before him, Gesner had described how
these fish were fashioned into "monsters." Here, Jonston's crowned Basilisk looks far less threatening than Pliny's
ancient "king of all snakes," whose poisonous breath not only killed everything in its vicinity, but could crumble the
hardest rocks.

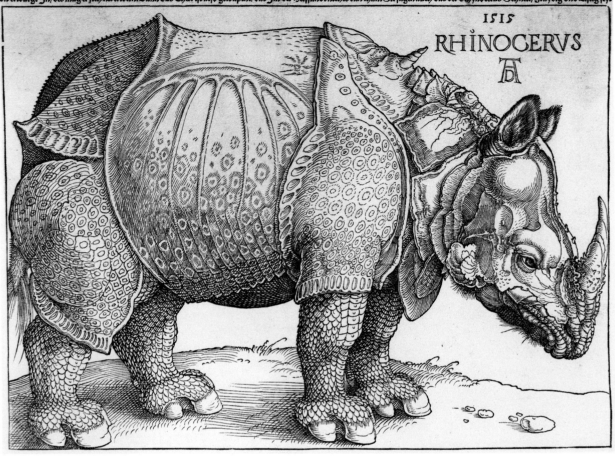

Nach Chriſtus gepurt.1513. Jar.Adi.j.May. hat man dem groß mechtigen Kunig von Portugall Emanuell gen Lyſabona pracht auß India/ein ſollich lebendig Thier. Das nennen ſie
Rhinocerus.Das iſt hye mit aller ſeiner geſtalt Abconderfet.Es hat ein farb wie ein geſpreckte Schildtkrot. Vnd iſt võ dicken Schalen vberlegt faſt feſt.Vnd iſt in der gröſß als der Helffandt
Aber nydertrechtiger von paynen/vnd faſt werhafftig. Es hat ein ſcharff ſtarck Horn vorn auff der naſen/Das begyndt es allweg zu wetzen wo es bey ſtaynen iſt.Das doſig Thier iſt des Helf=
fantz todt feyndt.Der Helffandt furcht es faſt vbel/dann wo es Jn ankumbt/ſo laufft Jm das Thier mit dem kopff zwiſchen dye fordern payn/vnd reyſt den Helffandt vnden am pauch auff
vñ erwürgt Jn/des mag er ſich nit erwern.Dann das Thier iſt alſo gewapent/das Jm der Helffandt nichts kan thün.Sie ſagen auch das der Rhynocerus Schnell/ Fraydig vnd Liſtig ſey.

97 ▪ INDIAN RHINOCEROS *Rhinoceros unicornis*

"Rhinocerus." Woodcut by Albrecht Dürer (1515). ▪ The saga of "Dürer's Rhinoceros" is a famous example of the results of uncritical imitation. The great German master never saw a live rhinoceros, but instead based his woodcut on his drawing copied from a sketch made by a local artist of a rhinoceros brought to Lisbon earlier that year. Although superbly executed, the rendering is incorrect: circles decorate the armored plates, the legs are scaly, and there is an extra horn on the beast's shoulder. This image appears verbatim (although reversed) in Gesner and Topsell, and was recopied through the mid 1700s.

Tab: XI.

Onager Aldro.: Wald Esel.

Monoceros seu Unicornu Iubatus.
Einhorn mit Mähnen.

Monoceros seu Unicornu aliud
Einhorn mit Mähnen ein andr art

98 · THREE UNICORNS

"Onager Aldro.; Monoceros seu Unicornu Iubatus; Monoceros seu Unicornu aliud." Engraving, by Matthaeus Merian from his own drawing. In *Historia naturalis de quadrupedibus . . .* by John Jonston (1655). ▪ Gesner had included the Unicorn in his *Historiae animalium* reluctantly and only because its magical "horn" was an item of commerce. Jonston, on the other hand, eagerly perpetuated the legend of this most famous of fabulous beasts and included several pages of depictions of variant types in his "Natural History." The top figure, based on a wild ass, has the horn of a rhinoceros and the feet of a hippopotamus; the central animal has cleft front hooves and either clawed or webbed hind feet; and the most horselike of the three also has cleft feet in the front and paws behind.

I^{ERE} SÉRIE. QUADRUPÈDES SANS OS MARSUPIAUX. (Is.G.S^tHil.)

8ème Ordre   { 1. *Fourmilier didactyle.* (Myrmecophaga didactyla, Lin.) ²⁄₇ de gr. nat.
ÉDENTÉS   { 2. *Fourmilier tamanoir.* (Myrmecophaga jubata, Buff.) ¼₃ de gr. natur.

99 ▪ GIANT ANTEATER *Myrmecophaga tridactyla* ▪ SILKY ANTEATER *Cyclopes didactylus*

"Fourmilier didactyle; Fourmilier tamanoir." Hand-colored etching, by Fournier from drawing by Edouard Traviès. In *Dictionnaire Universel d'Histoire Naturelle* edited by Alcide Dessalines d'Orbigny (1839–49). ▪ D'Orbigny supervised many of the best naturalists, artists, and engravers of the period in the production of the sixteen-volume *Dictionnaire*, which has been called the "best illustrated encyclopedia of natural history." The terrestrial Giant Anteater and the tiny, arboreal Silky Anteater (not drawn to scale) are New World members of the Order Edentata, meaning "without teeth." Insects, chiefly ants and termites, are captured efficiently with their rapid flicking tongue, which is almost as long as the animal's body. The sharp foreclaws are used for defense and to tear apart insect nests.

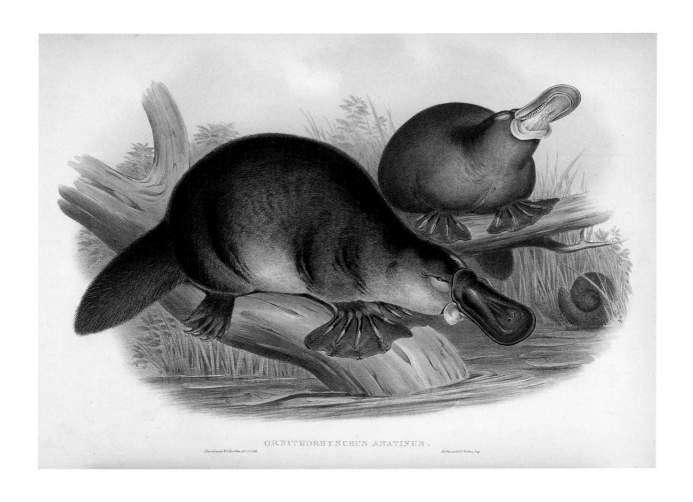

ORNITHORHYNCHUS ANATINUS.

J.Gould and H.C.Richter del et lith.   Hullmandel & Walton, Imp.

100 ▪ DUCKBILLED PLATYPUS *Ornithorhynchus anatinus*

"Ornithorhynchus anatinus." Hand-colored lithograph, by John Gould and H. C. Richter. In *The mammals of Australia* by John Gould (1845–63). ▪ A hoax was suspected when British zoologist George Shaw first described the Platypus in 1799 in his *Naturalist's Miscellany*. Until a live specimen was seen it was thought that parts of a mammal and a bird had been sewn together to create an improbable creature. Nearly fifty years later, John Gould depicted the Platypus and many more unusual Australian animals. This aquatic mammal has a ducklike bill, webbed and clawed feet, fur, and hatches its young from eggs and then nourishes them with milk.

BIBLIOGRAPHY OF
WORKS ILLUSTRATED

Basic sources consulted on zoological illustration were David Knight's *Zoological Illustration* (1977), S. Peter Dance's *Art of Natural History* (c. 1978), and Handasyde Buchanan's *Nature into Art* (1979). Chief among the many titles consulted frequently for biographical, historical, and zoological information were Bernhard Grzimek's *Animal Life Encyclopedia* (1972–, 1990), the Peterson and Audubon Society series of field guides, Willy Ley's *Dawn of Zoology* (1968), Joseph Wood Krutch's *World of Animals* (1961), and the 11th edition of the *Encyclopaedia Britannica* (1911). ▪ The recent edition of Sotheby's catalogues documenting the private library of the collector H. Bradley Martin are works of monumental scholarship. The two volumes from this group cited below as references were invaluable in all aspects of my research. ▪ Names of artists and craftspersons have been supplied whenever reasonably possible. When not indicated otherwise the artist engraved/lithographed his/her own drawings.

References Cited:

NISSEN, CLAUS. *Die botanische Buchillustration.* Stuttgart, 1952, 1966. [Hereafter *Nissen BBI*]

NISSEN, CLAUS. *Die zoologische Buchillustration.* Stuttgart, 1966–. [Hereafter *Nissen ZBI*]

SOTHEBY'S. *The library of H. Bradley Martin. Pt. 2. Magnificent color-plate ornithology.* New York: Sotheby's, 1989. [Hereafter *Martin 2*]

SOTHEBY'S. *The library of H. Bradley Martin. Pt. 5. Highly important and scientific ornithology.* New York: Sotheby's, 1989. [Hereafter *Martin 5*]

AGASSIZ, LOUIS. *Contributions to the natural history of the United States of America.* 4 vols. Boston: Little, Brown, 1857–62. ▪ 77 uncolored and partly hand-colored lithographs by A. Sonrel from drawings by Jacques Burkhardt and others. ▪ *Ref: Nissen ZBI 37.*

ALDROVANDI, ULISSE. *Opera omnia.* 13 vols. Bologna, 1599–1668. ▪ Woodcuts in text, by Cristoforo and G. B. Coriolanus from drawings by Lorenzo Bennini, Jacopo Ligozzi, Cornelius Swint, and others. ▪ *Ref: Nissen ZBI 72.*

AUDUBON, JOHN JAMES, and JOHN BACHMAN. *The quadrupeds of North America.* 3 vols. New York: V. G. Audubon, 1849–54. ▪ 155 hand-colored lithographs by R. Trembley from drawings by J. J. Audubon and John Woodhouse Audubon. ▪ *Ref: Nissen ZBI 163.*

BARBUT, JAMES. *Les genres des insectes de Linné; constates par divers enchantillons d'insectes d'Angleterre....* (Trans. of Barbut's *Genera insectorum* ..., 1780.) London: Dixwell, 1781. ▪ 22 hand-colored engravings from drawings by James Barbut. ▪ *Ref: Nissen ZBI 220.*

BARROW, JOHN HENRY. *Characteristic sketches of animals, principally in the zoological gardens, Regent's Park, drawn from the life and engraved by Thomas Landseer....* London: Zoological Society, 1832. ▪ 32 etchings, 32 etched vignettes by Thomas Landseer. ▪ *Ref: Nissen ZBI 240.*

BEWICK, THOMAS. *A general history of quadrupeds.* 8th ed. Newcastle, 1824. ▪ Wood engravings in the text by Thomas Bewick. ▪ *Ref: Nissen ZBI 351.*

BINGLEY, WILLIAM. *Memoirs of British quadrupeds, illustrative principally of their habits of life, instincts, sagacity, and uses to mankind....* London: Darton and Harvey, 1809. ▪ 71 etchings from drawings by Samuel Howitt. ▪ *Ref: Nissen ZBI 366.*

BONAPARTE, CHARLES-LUCIEN-JULES-LAURENT. *Iconografia della fauna italica per le quattro classi degli animali vertebrati.* 3 vols. Rome: Salviucci, 1832–41. ▪ 180 hand-colored lithographs by Battistelli from drawings by Carlos Ruspi, Petrus Quatrocchi, and Alexander Capalti. ▪ *Ref: Martin 2/48.*

BORKHAUSEN, MORITZ B. ET AL. *Teutsche Ornithologie....* Darmstadt, 1800–17. ▪ 132 hand-colored etchings by J. C. Susemihl and family and others. ▪ *Ref: Martin 2/53.*

BOURJOT SAINT-HILAIRE, ALEXANDRE. *Histoire naturelle des perroquets, troisième volume (supplémentaire) pour faire suite aux deux volumes de Levaillant.* Paris: Levrault, 1837–38. ▪ 111 hand-colored lithographs by Lemercier from drawings by Johann Carl Werner. ▪ *Ref: Martin 2/52.*

BUFFON, GEORGE-LOUIS LECLERCQ, COMTE DE. *Histoire naturelle, générale et particulière....* 44 vols. Vol. 38, *Quadrupèdes I (1788).* Paris: L'Imprimerie Royale, 1746–1804. ▪ Etchings from drawings by Jacques DeSève. ▪ *Ref: Nissen ZBI 672.*

———. *Histoire naturelle....* 127 vols. Vol. 28, *Quadrupèdes VII. (1800).* Paris: Dufart, 1799–1808. ▪ Etchings by Demanchy, Bequoy, and others from drawings by Jacques DeSève and Jacques Barraband. ▪ *Ref: Nissen ZBI 682.*

BURMEISTER, HERMANN. *Erläuterungen zur Fauna Brasiliens....* Berlin: George Reimer, 1856. ▪ 32 uncolored and hand-colored lithographs by Hugo Troschel and A. Rohlfs from drawings by Hermann Burmeister. ▪ *Ref: Nissen ZBI 761.*

CATESBY, MARK. *The Natural History of Carolina, Florida and the Bahama Islands: containing the figures of Birds, Beasts, Fishes, Serpents, Insects and Plants ... Together with their descriptions in English and French....* 2d ed. edited by George Edwards. 2 vols. London: Marsh, 1754. ▪ 220 hand-colored etchings: 217 by Mark Catesby, 3 by George D. Ehret. ▪ *Ref: Martin 2/65.*

CRAMER, PIETER. *Sammlung und Beschreibung ausländischer Schmetterlinge....* Nuremberg: Seligmann, 1788. ▪ Hand-colored engravings from drawings by Pieter Cramer. ▪ *Ref: Nissen ZBI 986 (1774 ed.)*

DANIELL, WILLIAM. *Interesting selections from animated nature with illustrative scenery.* 2 vols. London: Cadell & Davies, 1809. ▪ 120 monochrome aquatints by William Daniell. ▪ *Ref: Nissen ZBI 1040.*

DESCOURTILZ, JEAN T. *Ornithologie brésilienne ou histoire des oiseaux du Brésil....* Rio de Janeiro: Thomas Reeves, 1852, 1854–56. ▪ 12 chromolithographs by Jean T. Descourtilz. ▪ *Ref: Martin 2/69.*

DONOVAN, EDWARD. *The Natural History of British Quadrupeds....* 3 vols. in 2. London, 1820. ▪ 72 hand-colored etchings by Edward Donovan. ▪ *Ref: Nissen ZBI 1146.*

DÜRER, ALBRECHT. "Rhinocerus." Woodcut, 1515.

EDWARDS, WILLIAM HENRY. *The butterflies of North America.* 2d series. 3 vols. Boston, 1868–97. ▪ 154 hand-colored lithographs from drawings by Mary Peart. ▪ *Ref: Nissen ZBI 1234.*

EISENBERG, REIS, LE BARON D'. *L'anti-maquignonage pour éviter la surprise dans l'emplette des chevaux.* Amsterdam, Leipzig, 1764. ▪ Unsigned engravings. Spine reads: *L'art du manège.* ▪ *Ref: Nissen ZBI 1266.*

Encyclopédie méthodique.... 196(?) vols. Vol. 135, *Mammalogie, ou Description des espèces de mammifères ...* by Anselme-Gaetan Desmarest (1820–22). Paris: Meuve, Agasse, 1774–1832(?). ▪ 126 engravings from drawings by Jacques DeSève. ▪ *Ref: Nissen ZBI 4621.*

FAYRER, JOSEPH. *The thanatophidia of India....* 2d ed. London: Churchill, 1874. ▪ 31 chromolithographs from drawings by students of the Government School of Art, Calcutta. ▪ *Ref: Nissen ZBI 1339.*

GESNER, CONRAD. *Historiae animalium.* 5 vols. in 3. Zurich: Christopher Froschauer, 1551–87. ▪ Woodcuts in the text by the Workshop of Christopher Froschauer from anonymous and/or unsigned drawings. *Ref: Martin 5/1572.*

GOULD, JOHN. *The mammals of Australia.* 3 vols. London, 1845–63. ▪ 182 hand-colored lithographs by John Gould, Henry Constantine Richter, and Josef Wolf. ▪ *Ref: Nissen ZBI 1661.*

———. *A monograph of the macropodidae, or family of kangaroos.* London, 1841–42. ▪ 30 hand-colored lithographs by Henry Constantine Richter. ▪ *Ref: Nissen ZBI 1662.*

GRANDIDIER, ALFRED, and ALPHONSE MILNE EDWARDS. *Histoire physique, naturelle et politique de Madagascar....* 29 vols. in 50. Vol. 10, *Histoire naturelle des mammifères (atlas vol. 2, 1890).* Paris: L'Imprimerie Nationale, 1875–1942. ▪ 36 chromolithographs by John Gerrard Keulemans. ▪ *Ref: Nissen ZBI 1676.*

GRAY, JOHN EDWARD. *Tortoises, terrapins and turtles drawn from life....* London: Sotheran, 1872. ▪ 60 hand-colored lithographs by Edward Lear from drawings by James De Carle Sowerby. ▪ *Ref: Nissen ZBI 1701.*

———, and THOMAS HARDWICKE. *Illustrations of Indian Zoology; chiefly selected from the Collection of Major-General Hardwicke.* 2 vols. London: Richter, 1830–34. ▪ 166 hand-colored lithographs by Benjamin Waterhouse Hawkins; 36 hand-colored engravings by J. Swain from drawings by Waterhouse Hawkins. ▪ *Ref: Nissen ZBI 1694.*

HARRIS, MOSES. *The Aurelian, or Natural History of English Moths, and Butterflies, together with the Figures of their transformations and of the plants on which they feed.* 2d ed. London: Bohn, 1840. ▪ 44 hand-colored etchings by Moses Harris. ▪ *Ref: Nissen ZBI 1835.*

HEWITSON, WILLIAM CHAPMAN. *Specimens of a catalogue of Lycaenidae in the British Museum.* London: British Museum (Natural History) Zoology Dept., 1862. ▪ 8 hand-colored lithographs by William Chapman Hewitson. ▪ *Ref: Nissen ZBI 1931.*

HOLBROOK, JOHN EDWARD. *North American herpetology; or A description of the reptiles inhabiting the United States.* 2d ed. 5 vols. London: R. Baldwin, 1842. ▪ Hand-colored lithographs and chromolithographs by George Lehman and P. S. Duval from drawings by J. Sera and John H. Richards. ▪ *Ref: Nissen ZBI 1980.*

JONSTON, JOHN. *Historia naturalis de Insectis libri III . . . de Serpentibus . . . libri II. . . .* Frankfort, 1653. ▪ Engravings by Matthaeus Merian, the Younger. ▪ *Ref: Nissen ZBI 2135.*

———. *Historia naturalis de quadrupedibus. . . .* Frankfort, 1655. ▪ Engravings by Matthaeus Merian, the Younger. ▪ *Ref: Nissen ZBI 2131 (eds. of 1650, 1657).*

LAWRENCE, JOHN. *History and delineation of the horse, in all his varieties.* London: Albion, 1809. ▪ 11 engravings and frontispiece from drawings chiefly by Benjamin Marshall and George Stubbs. ▪ *Ref: Nissen ZBI 2397.*

LOW, DAVID. *The Breeds of the domestic animals of the British Islands. . . .* 2 vols. London: Longmans, 1842. ▪ Hand-colored lithographs by Thomas Fairland from drawings by William Nicholson, after paintings by William Shiels. ▪ *Ref: Nissen ZBI 2564.*

LYDEKKER, RICHARD. *Wild oxen, sheep, and goats of all lands, living and extinct.* London: Rowland Ward, 1898. ▪ 65 illustrations, including 28 chromolithographs by Josef Wolf and Joseph Smit. ▪ *Ref: Nissen ZBI 2614.*

MARÉCHAL, NICOLAS, BERNARD-GERMAIN-ETIENNE DE LA VILLE, LE COMTE DE LACÉPÈDE, and GEORGES CUVIER. *La Ménagerie du Muséum National d'Histoire Naturelle, ou les animaux vivants. . . .* Paris: Dentu, 1801. ▪ 39 etchings by Simon Charles Miger from paintings by Nicolas Maréchal. ▪ *Ref: Nissen ZBI 2353.*

MERIAN, MARIA SIBYLLA. *Dissertation sur la génération et les trans-formations des insectes de Surinam. . . .* 2d ed. The Hague: Gosse, 1726. ▪ 72 hand-colored etchings from drawings chiefly by Maria Sibylla Merian. ▪ *Ref: Nissen BBI 1341.*

NILSSON, SVEN. *Illuminerade Figurer till Skandinaviens Fauna.* 2 vols. Lund: Berling, 1832–40. ▪ 200 hand-colored lithographs by C. Scheele and others, from drawings by Magnus Köerner, M. v. Wright, and others. ▪ *Ref: Martin 5/1756.*

NOZEMAN, CORNELIUS, MARTINUS HOUTTUYN, and JAN CHRISTIAN SEPP. *Nederlandsche vogelen. . . .* 5 vols. Amsterdam: Sepp, 1770–1829. ▪ 255 hand-colored engravings with etching by members of Sepp family. ▪ *Ref: Martin 2/172.*

ORBIGNY, ALCIDE-CHARLES-DESSALINES D', ed. *Dictionnaire uni-versel d'histoire naturelle.* 16 vols. 3 vols. *Atlas.* Paris, 1839–49. ▪ 288 hand-colored etchings by Fournier, Baudran Annedouche, L. Legrand, and others, from drawings by Edouard Traviès, Paul Louis Oudart, Jean Gabriel Prêtre, Johann Carl Werner, Auguste Vaillant, and others. ▪ *Ref: Martin 5/1769.*

PALLAS, PETER SIMON. *Novae species quadrupedum, e glirium or-dine. . . .* Erlangen: Wolfgang Walther, 1778–79. ▪ 71 engrav-ings in two states, 39 uncolored, 32 hand-colored, by several engravers from drawings by several artists. ▪ *Ref: Nissen ZBI 3074.*

PISO, WILLEM, and GEORGES MARCGRAVE. *Historia naturalis brasiliae auspicio et beneficio illustratis. . . .* 2d ed. Amsterdam, 1658. ▪ Woodcuts in text, unsigned. ▪ *Ref: Martin 5/1802, 1803 (1st and var. eds.)*

ROESEL VON ROSENHOF, AUGUSTIN. *Der Monatlich Herausgegeben Insectenbelustigung. . . .* 4 vols. Nuremburg, 1746–61. ▪ Hand-colored etchings by Augustin Roesel von Rosenhof. ▪ *Ref: Nissen ZBI 3466.*

SCHLEGEL, HERMANN. *Abbildungen neuer oder unvollständig bekannter Amphibien. . . .* 2 vols. (text, plates). Düsseldorf: Arnz, 1837–44. ▪ 50 hand-colored lithographs by several litho-graphers from drawings by several artists. ▪ *Ref: Nissen ZBI 3680.*

SCHREBER, JOHANN CHRISTIAN DANIEL. *Die Saugethiere in Ab-bildungen nach der Natur. . . .* ▪ A collection of more than 100 original watercolors, most unsigned, others signed by various artists, made as either original drawings for, or copies from, illustrations that appeared in *Die Saugethiere . . .* , Erlangen, 1774(?)–1855(?). ▪ *Ref: Nissen ZBI 3748.*

SEBA, ALBERT. *Locupletissimi rerum naturalium thesauri. . . .* 4 vols. Amsterdam: Jansson, Waesberg, 1734–65. ▪ 449 etchings. ▪ *Ref: Nissen ZBI 3793.*

SHAW, GEORGE. *Zoological lectures delivered at the Royal Institu-tion. . . .* 2 vols. London: Kearsley, 1809. ▪ 167 etchings by Smith, Heath, Griffith, Eastgate, and others from drawings by Moses Griffith. ▪ *Ref: Nissen ZBI 3837.*

SPIX, JOHANN BAPTIST VON. *Delectus animalium articulatorum. . . .* Munich, 1830–34. ▪ Hand-colored engravings by Wilhelm Siegrist from drawings by Eggard, Schach, Joseph Unger, and others. Spine reads: *Insecta Brasiliensa.* ▪ *Ref: Nissen ZBI 3949.*

TOPSELL, EDWARD. *History of four-footed beasts and serpents . . . with The theater of insects by T. Muffet. . . .* 2 vols. in 1. London, 1658. ▪ Engraved illustrations in the text. Translation and ad-aptation of portions of Gesner's *Historiae animalium.* ▪ *Ref: Nissen ZBI 4147.*

WILHELM, GOTTLIEB TOBIAS. *Unterhaltungen aus der Naturge-schichte.* 12 vols. Augsburg: Engelbrecht, 1792–1802. ▪ Hand-colored engravings by G. T. Wilhelm from his own drawings. ▪ *Ref: Nissen ZBI 4408 (27 vols., 1792–1834).*

WILSON, ALEXANDER. *American ornithology; or, The natural his-tory of birds in the United States.* 9 vols. Philadelphia: Bradford and Inskeep, 1808–14. ▪ 76 etchings by G. Murray, J. G. Warn-icke, and Alexander Lawson from drawings by Alexander Wilson. ▪ *Ref: Martin 2/232.*

WOOD, JOHN GEORGE. *Homes without hands: being a description of the habitations of animals classed according to their principles of construction.* 2d. ed. N.Y.: Appleton, 1866. ▪ Wood engravings and illustrations in the text by Mrs. G. Pearson, from drawings by Friedrich Wilhelm Keyl and Edgar Albert Smith. ▪ *Ref: Nissen ZBI 4445.*

Zoological Society of London. *Transactions.* 2d series. London: The Society, 1847–. Vol. 3, *Transactions* (1849). ▪ Hand-colored and uncolored lithographs by John Christian Zeitter and others, from drawings by Robert Hills and others. ▪ *Ref: Nissen ZBI 4788.*

INDEX

The original conception for an exhibition is the curator's only truly independent act. After that, the efforts of others are essential, beginning with the raw materials—the rich holdings of illustrated natural history books in the collections of The New York Public Library. ▪ Foremost among the many to whom I owe thanks is Bernard McTigue, Curator of the Arents Collections and Keeper of Rare Books, who ten years ago first invited me to prepare an exhibition, and has continued to offer down-to-earth encouragement and support. Richard Newman, Manager of Publications, has always cheered on my literary efforts. Thanks are due Beth Diefendorf, Chief of the General Research Division, for her ongoing support. ▪ Susan Saidenberg, Manager of the Exhibitions Program, and her entire talented staff all deserve praise: especially Jeanne Bornstein, Research Coordinator; Barbara Bergeron for her editorial skills; Exhibition Designer Lou Storey, and Head Preparator, Tracy Fell; Exhibitions Conservator Myriam de Arteni; Jeanne Mihich, Registrar; Melitte Buchman and all staff in the Registrars Office; Susan Rabbiner, Education Specialist; and Philip Mrozek, Exhibitions Assistant. Special thanks to Lawrence Murphy, who supervised the photography of the illustrations for this book, and to Heidi Stock of the Publications Office. I am grateful for special help given by Richard Hill and the staff at the Library at 43rd Street, especially Beatrice Dey; Elizabeth Bentley, Chief of the Science and Technology Research Center and her staff; my colleagues in the General Research Division; Robert Rainwater, Curator of the Spencer Collection; Roberta Waddell and the Print Room staff; the staffs of the Miriam and Ira D. Wallach Division of Art, Prints and Photographs, and the Rare Books and Manuscripts Division; and Helga Borck. ▪ I am indebted to the following who provided specialized assistance in the planning and preparation of the exhibition: Bonnie Rosenblum and Anne Irwin in the Public Affairs and Development Office; Carlee Drummer, Lauren Geiger Moye, and Donna Fields in the Public Relations Office; Marilan Lund and the staff of the Graphics Office; and Myrna Martin of the Volunteer Office. A great deal of innocent temerity is needed for an amateur to take on the entire animal kingdom. The assistance of several very helpful consultants from the American Museum of Natural History made it possible for me to complete this project. In addition to overseeing the bird illustrations Mary LeCroy generously recruited colleagues from other Museum departments: Marie Lawrence (Mammalogy), Michael Klemens (Herpetology), Louis Sorkin (Entomology), Norma Feinberg (Ichthyology), and Walter Sage (Invertebrates). It has been a pleasure as well as an education to work with these dedicated scientists. ▪ I am grateful to have had a new opportunity to collaborate with and learn from Joseph Kastner. Our editor, Ruth Peltason, deserves thanks for her professionalism and keen eye, and Elissa Ichiyasu has designed the book to enhance the beauty of the illustrations. ▪ The exhibition would not have been possible without the generous support of Bulgari and the Vincent Astor Foundation. ▪ My final thanks are for my husband, David, and sons, Andrew and Adam, who have (usually) graciously served as sounding-boards for the past three years.—*Miriam T. Gross*

ACKNOWLEDGMENTS

Tab. V.